ANGRY RAIN

ANGRY RAIN

a brief memoir

Maurice Kenny

EDITED AND WITH AN INTRODUCTION BY

DEREK C. MAUS

excelsior editions

AN IMPRINT OF STATE UNIVERSITY OF NEW YORK PRESS

Cover art: original color collage by Anna Neva, used by permission of the artist.

Different versions of portions of this book previously appeared in the following publications:
"Angry Rain: A Brief Autobiographical Memoir from Boyhood to College"
Contemporary Authors Autobiography Series 22. Detroit: Gale, 1995.
On Second Thought. Norman, OK: University of Oklahoma Press, 1995.

Published by
State University of New York Press, Albany

Printed in the United States of America

Excelsior Editions is an imprint of State University of New York Press

For information, contact State University of New York Press, Albany, NY
www.sunypress.edu

Library of Congress Cataloging-in-Publication Data

Names: Kenny, Maurice, 1929–2016, author. | Maus, Derek C., editor.
Title: Angry rain : a brief memoir / Maurice Kenny ; edited and with an introduction by Derek C. Maus.
Description: Albany : Excelsior Editions, an imprint of the State University of New York Press, [2018]
Identifiers: LCCN 2017049448| ISBN 9781438471068 (paperback : alk. paper) | ISBN 9781438471075 (e-book)
Subjects: LCSH: Kenny, Maurice, 1929–2016. | Authors, American—20th century—Biography. | Mohawk Indians—Biography.
Classification: LCC PS3561.E49 Z46 2018 | DDC 818/.5403 [B] —dc23
LC record available at https://lccn.loc.gov/2017049448

10 9 8 7 6 5 4 3 2 1

For Lorne Simon . . .

Whose life was cut short . . .
Of all the words he stored
In his imagination
Few got to paper in time . . .

In memory of . . .

Diane Burns, Diane Decorah, Peter Blue Cloud, Fred Hoch, Mary Dickson, JP, Rose C., Cathy B., Ms. Gertrude, Randy Lewis, Joseph White, Lorraine Wilson, Manny Bernstein, Tim Jock

. . . and especially my parents, Andy and Doris.

Contents

Introduction

As it turns out, Saint Petersburg in July is a great time and place to get editorial work done, especially when one is still dealing with jet lag after a transatlantic flight. I found this out during the summer of 2016 when I took advantage of the famed "White Nights" of that most literary of cities to work on finalizing the manuscript of the book you are holding in your hands. Although New York—a city that Maurice Kenny knew quite well, as you will read in the recollections that follow—was famously called "the city that never sleeps," Saint Petersburg's midsummer version has a legitimate claim on the title as well. On each of my visits there, I have marveled that one can make do with only three or four hours of sleep a night.

I was in Saint Petersburg that summer to teach in an international summer-school program—and had plenty of work to keep me busy in that context—but I had also brought the manuscript of Maurice's memoir with me to work on in my spare time, which is plentiful during the long days of the northern Russian summer. I recall with great fondness a particular sleepless night of editorial work in my rented fifth-floor apartment on Petrogradsky Island. The large windows of my preferred writing room overlooked the rooftops of the quarter both to the east and the west. As I passed a series of midnight hours with a frequently refreshed cup of tea and Maurice's words displayed on my laptop, I hardly noticed as the twilight streaming through the windows subtly shifted from my left side to my right, dusk almost imperceptibly transforming into dawn. I am very much a night owl and have always enjoyed drifting off to sleep as songbirds greet the rising sun; however, when that phenomenon occurs at three in the morning and is not preceded by a stretch of recognizable night, there is something rather uncanny about it. The indeterminate mood stimulated by my surroundings proved quite fitting for working on a book that swings through a wide arc of emotions, from warmth and joy to recrimination and regret. When I had recited Maurice's poem "Wild Strawberries" to a group of my Russian students, many of them remarked approvingly about his *russkaia dusha*—his "Russian soul"—and that somewhat metaphysical association played in my mind as I worked through the pages of his text in my twilit aerie.

Maurice and I had spent a lot of time together since I first made his acquaintance, so a lot of the individual stories that make up this memoir are ones that I had heard from him before reading them again as his editor. Whether performing on a stage, sharing a dinner-table, or riding in a car, Maurice was an ardent and gifted storyteller. In his poetry and prose, he often writes about and adopts the voice of other people, animals, plants, and sometimes even spirits. In his private recollections, though, he generally told stories in which he featured prominently, whether or not he was their protagonist. With many people, such a reflexive focus might seem narcissistic or vain, but Maurice had already amassed seven decades of life experiences by the time I met him, so he legitimately had a lot of tales to tell. And what a life it was! My own gallivanting through the world seemed so tame compared to the multiple cross-continental journeys he took aboard a series of Greyhound buses—he suffered from severe claustrophobia that made flying an emotional ordeal—in order to read his words aloud in small towns and giant cities alike.

In the late summer of 2001, I had just moved to Potsdam, New York, where I had landed my first academic job at SUNY Potsdam. I spent the days before the start of the semester in my new office, unloading books and meeting my colleagues, one of whom turned out to be a Mohawk poet whose name had cropped up here and there during my undergraduate and graduate studies. After a brief initial meeting in the hallway, Maurice started regularly walking the fifty or so feet down from his office to linger at my open door. One wall of my office was adorned with a large poster that featured John Coltrane's face, and during one of his visits Maurice tipped his chin toward the poster and casually mentioned that "John and Alice used to live close to me when they first met, and I'd talk to them out on the street a lot." Not long thereafter he told me the story—included in this memoir, of course—of how Orson Welles had whipped him off the running board of a hansom cab in Manhattan. I initially had my doubts about the veracity of some of these yarns, but they dissipated quickly. Although Maurice was certainly not above having a somewhat pliable memory about where, when, and in what order things happened, I learned that he *never* exaggerated when it came to the people he had met and known in his life—he didn't need to.

I started to grasp the extent of his notable acquaintances when Maurice invited me to his apartment and showed me—with his characteristic mix of pride and self-consciousness—some of the books that had been inscribed to him warmly and personally by their authors. I learned that Maurice had corresponded with, shared meals with, worked with, traveled with, lived with, and more than once fought with writers, actors, and artists that I had theretofore only known as names in anthologies, credits on a movie screen, or subjects on my doctoral exams. For a while, I would still jokingly chide him about dropping names when he mentioned his relationship with Amiri Baraka or Leslie Marmon Silko or Allen Ginsberg or Wendy Rose or Willard Motley or Simon Ortiz or Paddy Chayefsky or Audre Lorde or . . . (you get the point, right?). After getting to know him better, though, I realized that he wasn't putting on airs by listing his famous friends. He spoke with the same vivacity and depth when telling stories about the lesser-known (at least to me . . .) writers whose work he helped bring forth as a publisher with *Contact/II* and the Strawberry Press. Tellingly, he reserved some of his greatest enthusiasm for recounting the students with whom he had worked at the University of Oklahoma, at North Country Community College, at SUNY Potsdam, during his various residencies all over the continent, or at impromptu workshops after one of the thousands of readings that he gave during his career as a barnstorming poet. Maurice was not without his anxieties and he certainly was not uncritical in his interactions with other people, but I was quickly struck by the extent to which his relationships with people were marked by a depth that I envied; the richness of the stories he told (and frequently retold) through the years was a function of the intense attention that he paid to everyone who made it into his consciousness.

So much of this book is the fruit of that intense attention. He first told me about his desire to write his memoir while we were sitting on a train traveling from Prague to Berlin in the summer of 2012. He had put aside his deep-seated loathing of air travel to accept a series of invitations to read his work in southern Germany and in Belgium, and when he invited me along to serve as what he called his "combination of Sherpa and hype-man," I suggested we use the opportunity to visit the cities of Franz Kafka and Marlene Dietrich (two artists he revered, albeit for very different reasons). During the six-hour journey on the comfortable German train, he strung together a series of recollections for me. I'd heard some of them before, but others were new to me and departed from his usual recollections about sharing a stage with Margaret Atwood at the MLA convention or traveling through Mexico as a younger man with only a pocketful of coins and limited Spanish. Perhaps he was still under the influence of our trip to the Kafka Museum in Prague as he told me about violent confrontations, about painfully lost loves, about betrayals, and about reversals of fortune. These did not cancel out the generally happy stories I had heard from him previously, but they gave a clearer focus to my picture of his life, of the sourness that can linger amid success, of the immense creative power that arises in equal measure out of grief and elation. His vitality on that trip astounded me; I will never forget the reading he gave in Regensburg despite having been awake and without clean clothes (thanks, Air France!) for the better part of two full days. He was eighty-two years old at the time and I had begun to think he might simply choose to live forever, but some part of him obviously reckoned his remaining days more sagely. As we sat in that train, eating cherries and looking at the countryside whizzing by, he made it very clear to me that he wanted to commit the memories he was sharing with me to writing while he still could.

He completed the full manuscript for *Angry Rain* by autumn of 2015, thanks to some long days and evenings of collaborative work with two talented young scholars from SUNY Potsdam, Jeannette Godreau and Kevin Bertolero. Sadly, his health was already starting to worsen by this point, and the Saturdays and Sundays during which they helped him transcribe his thoughts into his computer—which he invariably referred to as "that infernal machine"—were as often spent conversing about life and literature as working on the book. He no longer had the stamina to write for hours without a break that he had during the time in which he produced the notebooks, legal pads, and teetering piles of paper full of his handwritten words that packed every nook and cranny of the spare bedroom in his Saranac Lake apartment. I will always be grateful for the care and precocious sagacity with which Jeanette and Kevin treated both Maurice's person and his words while preparing the first full draft of this memoir. I can assert without hesitation that it would not exist without them.

Upon Maurice's death on April 16, 2016, the task of preparing the manuscript for publication fell to me. As we sat on the train to Berlin, I had promised that I would take on this work if the necessity arose, and now it was time to make good on that promise. The two external readers who had reviewed the manuscript for the press were both generally enthusiastic about it; however, they were also equally insistent that there needed to be some fairly significant changes made to its structure and to its content before it was ready for publication. Maurice had received these comments about two months before his death and we had (thankfully) spoken briefly about how he wanted to address them just before he went into the hospital for what would, alas, be the final time. These conversations guided me as I struggled to establish my sense of his authorial intent. It would have been simple enough to impose a strict chronological order on the telling of his story, but *Angry Rain* is not a history textbook, it is a memoir; preserving the narrative quality of a story being told as it is remembered is, in my view, absolutely essential in such a work. Without cutting any of his digressions out entirely, I did rearrange some of them to make the interconnections among the various chapters and subchapters feel a little less disjointed. As a writer fond of both ellipsis and caesura, Maurice very intentionally fragments the expression of his thoughts in both his prose and his poetry. Out of a desire to retain this fragmentation at the atomic level, I retained his often-idiosyncratic punctuation and usage at the molecular level of phrases, sentences, and paragraphs, though I also made some macroscopic adjustments in the ordering and arrangement of larger sections of the manuscript. I am firmly convinced that these changes in no way damage either the style or substance of his words; such an injury would be unconscionable to me. Rather, the moves I made were akin to shifting around the furnishings of an already well-appointed room to improve its *feng shui.* Maurice provided more than enough *qi* (if I may belabor my metaphor . . .) on his own to vivify the book without any additions on my part.

To close, a brief word about the nature of the truth of these recollections: Maurice's memory as a storyteller was both immense and fraught with what is often euphemized as "poetic license." As noted earlier, I never knew him to fabricate memories, but his penchant for rearranging details into a story that made sense *to him* became very apparent to me at times while editing this book. I feel secure of my ability to spot this process happening partly because I saw him use it more than once in recounting events at which I was present. For example, after our trip to Europe in 2012, he came back to Upstate New York full of new tales, whether about the beauty of the linden trees of Berlin, about reading his poems aloud at Rimbaud's grave in northern France, or about bickering impishly with the cantankerous waiter in a seaside café in Barcelona. One of the stories he told with great glee involved a radiant woman in a dark green dress who passed by on the sidewalk as he and I sipped coffee and blathered on about Kafka during an evening in the old city of Prague. He went so far as to turn this story into a poem that he read with impish delight in the middle of the Adirondack winter that followed our trip:

The Czech Lady of the Evening (Enchantment)

She stood tall in her whispering gown
which early night breezes blew
tight to her thigh. Derek, I called.
See this beautiful creature standing alone
under this July moon in Praha. We were
together there having coffee on our last night in
this crazy city . . . one of the more beautiful in the world.
We went mainly to discover Kafka,
a famed historical synagogue, an enormous
castle, and my friend to a fun burlesque.
                    But I'm forgetting my story.
We sat at an open air café, sipping coffee,
chatting, I thinking about our train ride

to Berlin early on the morrow when I
did spot this Venus of night in her
emerald gown rising on air, billowing
about her figure, a Greek statue,
attempting to catch Derek's gaze to this
stunning beauty who stood in the light
of that Republic moon alone, alone I said,
without an escort, free to the world.
No, no, I doubt she was hooking, she was
a classic example of music, of poetry, of love,
of beauty with staggering innocence, purity.
Oh to have a brush and paint this phantom
in all her glory for the world and time to know
eternally.
But I guess he was busy watching
a moth flutter about the street lamp,
his hearing the last Beethoven
concerto . . . which is also a thing of beauty,
but this heavenly, glamorous young
woman . . . stands there waiting for love,
for a handsome young man to arrive,
sweep this damsel off to his castle forever
to be his bride and queen.
Derek's response,
I'd better take off for my show soon as it
starts at ten. She crossed a busy street
away from the lamp's light and eyes
of an older tourist much too late in time.

Not a word of the story that Maurice told—in prose or in verse—about this episode was untrue . . . and yet little, if any, of the story that he told was particularly accurate from a historian's perspective either. Three nights' worth of experiences in Prague intertwined among each other (with a snippet from a later night in Berlin borrowed in for good measure . . .) in his story, and the location gradually shifted from a nondescript café in the riverside Malá Strana quarter to Prague Castle, high on its promontory overlooking the city. After the fourth time I heard our mutual experience retold in this manner, I gave up bothering to quibble about the details I knew to be inaccurate; the tale he told was far from "wrong" in capturing the mood of our Czech sojourn or the tenor of our thoughts upon the occasion. It was *his* memory of the moment and it made for a great story, albeit one that would be inadmissible in court.

I do not wish the reader to infer from this that I believe this book to be the product of either deliberate misrepresentation or the failing memory of an aging and increasingly ill man. Guile was not a feature of Maurice's personality during the years I knew him (others can speak for the first seventy years of his life), and I would be happy beyond measure to retain my wits as well as he did into his mid-eighties. Rather, I would urge readers to accept his words with the same sensibility that I tried to bring to their editing: these are the thoughts of a man who is not particularly interested in trying to "sell" a particular image of himself, but rather trying to come to terms with the ways in which a number of different incidents—some good, some terrible—affected who and what he became. When he refers to his lifelong scorn for John Crowe Ransom's rejection of his early work (and I can vouch for the fact that Maurice kept and looked at Ransom's letter regularly), I ask you to consider it within the context of the myriad other rebuffs—physical and emotional—about which he writes. Similarly, when you see the lightness and warmth with which he writes about the flowers that grew on the riverbanks near his childhood home or the friendships he made while working at the Marboro bookstore in Manhattan, recognize that they are an integral reflection of the poet who could almost salaciously praise the taste of wild strawberries while simultaneously reminding you of the blood and tears that make your store-bought strawberries taste so foul by comparison. At some point during those long nights of editing in Saint Petersburg, I simply stopped asking whether any given detail of what I was editing was accurate; I had to adopt a perspective akin to that of the rooftop pigeons who snoozed outside my windows as I worked (I cannot claim for myself the eagle's feathers that honor his artistic mastery). This additional breadth-of-view—and perhaps distance as well—allowed me to recognize a truth far more compelling than that conveyed by strict factual verisimilitude: this book is the living, perhaps imperfect memory of an indomitable—and yet also profoundly wounded—artist whose absence I have mourned every day since his passing.

Nia:wen, Maurice, for the chance to finish carrying these words into print.

—DEREK C. MAUS

Preface

Mountains surround me; white pine, hemlock, spruce, birch, the ever-beautiful tamarack; a coyote howls out of the night darkness; raccoons scurry up and down the hills near the house; a bear nibbles blueberries and blackberries; chipmunks cache their winter foods under the porch; a female cardinal alights on telephone wires; a crow caws in upper branches of an elm; a loon calls; a red-tailed hawk wheels over the village below where a river gurgles and sings you to sleep across balmy nights. Pansies and forget-me-nots, hawkweed and day lilies brighten the morning as sun rises east behind a mountain range to slowly drift south.

The Adirondacks. The High Peaks. Maple Hill.

I'm home. My blood family not too far away, my surrogate son Dean easily . . . if only electronically . . . reachable through this machine. Friends are all so close I could call down the hill to them in an emergency.

Adirondacks. Saranac Lake, woods and lakes, flowers and animals, birds, the great and handsome mountains are here around me. Sweetgrass is braided and hangs from the wall; sage is in the drawer of the chest for burning if needed. When winter blizzards come, snow will pile up to windows and all trees shall flower with white.

Long travels are finished, new lands explored; friends and acquaintances have come and gone in the light of day and dark of evening. Mexico, the Caribbean, the Virgin Islands, British Columbia are over, the past, deep in memory and the thrills they gifted. New York City, Chicago, San Francisco are blots on the map . . . no longer necessary. Onchiota and Bloomingdale are more important to everyday living. The hardware store and the Price Chopper offer more surprises than Boston or San Juan . . . now. These days Mexico City and Vancouver, El Paso and Tucson, St. Thomas and Trinidad, Campeche, the Yucatan, Barbados and Martinique, Berlin and Barcelona, Paris and Prague, Graz and Namur, colorful, fruitful, some bejeweled, others crawling with poverty . . . they no longer offer an incentive to roam. The wanderlust has cooled, as awe-inspiring as travel has always been, will always be. The feet don't itch, the eye is dulled, the spirit is weakened. The cool summer porch is more comforting; the winter supper in the kitchen . . . a chicken roasting in the oven, potatoes boiling on the burner, folks busy tearing lettuce for a salad and slicing tomatoes and mushrooms. The handshake is there, good morning rests on the lips, the church bells chime, sirens blow, canoe paddles down the lake, river rushes over the dam, birds chirp, the Queen (my house cat) meows, mice scratch, the blare of reggae hurtles out of the Waterhole, the library loans books, Mrs. Petty jams her jellies, Emily refinishes her huge kitchen, Pendragon puts on another play, kids skate on the frozen lake, and artists chip huge blocks of ice and stack them into a castle of a winter fairyland festival for the annual carnival.

The Adirondacks, the High Peaks, Maple Hill, home.

In the novel *As I Lay Dying*, Addie Bundren suggests that she was violated by life; in her case, it was her sense of aloneness that was violated, both in the sense of solitude and isolation. The Lakota holy man Black Elk once said that we human beings must celebrate the greening of the day. I have celebrated that green spring and flowery summer, that russet autumn and snowy January. I have also been violated by, and in turn violated, life. The violation and the celebration have produced hundreds of poems and stories and made me acquainted with the night, the day, and more human beings than I can possibly remember, humans who have dallied with my mind, body, and spirit, the creative process and the roast venison on my table; humans who have brought great pleasures to my many mornings, and burning pain to my darkest hours. Humans who have offered a way, a door, and those who stood as a wall forbidding passage. Some will be remembered always, others are best forgotten as quickly as the rabbit hops into the bramble, the mole into its hole, the fox through wild grapes. Many are remembered here on this paper . . . those who deserve remembering from my childhood and young life.

No marigold grows without rain and sunshine, nor stalwart white pine, nor any child. Nor can a writer grow out of childhood joys and miseries without the rain of family and friends and the sunshine of the Creator of the worlds. I am no different from anyone else . . . farmers, mountain guides, trackers, students, teachers, poets, highwaymen, window dressers, clerks, bank tellers, priests, visionaries, garbage collectors (who have always been some of my favorite conversationalists), the old men on the park benches, the elderly spinsters offering bread crusts to pigeons or squirrels. I too have offered crusts; I sit on the park bench and talk now with students, with bank tellers, waiters from the local lunch counters and bars. I stroll through shadows and apparitions of those who came here to the mountains surrounding Saranac Lake to cure or to die in a tubercular cough at the Trudeau sanitoriums. I live in a house with a boy-ghost who died in poverty of lung and home. He is swaddled in black cloth, choking in a white shirt buttoned tightly at the collar . . . he comes at night and sometimes rocks in the rocking chair. What does he want to say, reveal, complain about? I must listen and write his story in a poem or fiction. I must listen the same way I have always listened to the voices that moved around me in dreams or nightmares, on the streets or in the classrooms where I have walked and talked, spoken to innocent minds . . . as though my mind was a receptacle, an archive of valued information. Listening we learn, and we learn from dreams and the ghosts and the presences who visit us in the tombs in which we all live. Only a few are successful in breaking out of those tombs or through those walls that surround us, making captives of our minds and spirits.

Damn, I have been lucky, fortunate that there have been so many to give me the pick to break down walls, break open the tomb, the grave in which so many of us spend our lives. Wanda put the pick in my hands, as did Werner Beyer, Douglas Angus, Mary and Fred, Josh, Joe and Jimmy, the horses I rode, the river I canoed or strolled along, the mountains I hiked. Mexico opened doors, as did St. Thomas, as did Indiana and Brooklyn . . . as did even the humble Potsdam that's not the one near linden-lined and history-haunted Berlin. Paul and Ruth, Larry and the Brownings, Pete and Rokwaho . . . dear people who haunt the dream world, some of whom like Lorne and Donna have been released into the echo of life, and some who remain on the right and left shoulder blade whispering, ever whispering . . . Rocco and Cigar, Aunt Flo and Etta, Uncle Jim who probably first teased me with the possible ownership of a horse. To all of them I am so very grateful for the wondrous gifts brought to my hands and my imagination.

Surely I am indebted more to the beauties of Mother Earth than any other spirit. Surely my deepest of gratitude goes to my father, who saw that I survived in the violent world, and to my mother, who brought me into the green celebration of life, and to my sisters, who stung me into celebrating ceremony and violence. Surely I owe a deep and abiding debt to Quino, who brought such hell into my young manhood but gave gloss to the produce of my pen. I know the love that my niece Martha has always given, as well as the joy and fun, so surely I owe her much and I am thankful we are friends. I owe the winds, the rain, the roving clouds, the moon who has protected me all these years the way all grandmothers protect their children. I owe the stars, the waters, the turtle who held me on his back. I owe the beautiful poems of Wendy and Simon and Peter, whose blue cloud, like Dan's soft wolf robe, has comforted and replenished; and the foods of George and Rochelle . . . their pear tree and their often funny words; and the generous words of Sarah and Frank, and Chad and Dan, and my beautiful Lori, who left us for the other world, and Jen, who lent so much love and loyalty. They have given to me from their life-spirit, their life-blood, to excess.

Rain has fallen in torrents, but it has always been followed by sun. Blizzards have tormented but were also followed by a warm breeze. Waters have always flowed in the river and quenched a terrible thirst, exhilarated, stimulated, activated.

The Adirondacks, the High Peaks, Saranac Lake, home.

A special thanks to Wanda McCaddon and Julian Block. Additional thanks to Sharon Offner of The Writer's Voice of The Silver Bay Association; Deborah Ott of Just Buffalo Literary Center; Jeannette Armstrong of the En'owkin Centre in British Columbia; Paul Smith's College; Poets & Writers; the Native Writers' Circle of the Americas; the Lila Wallace Foundation; the Lannan Foundation; the Empire State Center for the Book, and their New York State Writers Hall of Fame; everyone at the Maison de la Poésie in Namur; Dennis and Elaine Maloney of White Pine Press; Derek Maus and Stephanie Tritt; Dan Bodah and all the generations of his family; John and Eva Fadden and their sons; John Radigan and Cheryl Culotta; Carol Vossler; Tim and Diana Fortune; Chad and Jen Sweeney; Randy Burns; Caroline Hotaling and her parents, Jim and Mary; Penny Kelsey and Levi; Dean Roczen; Phil Gallos and Sharon O'Brien; Neil Surprenant; Tony and Lynn Waickman; Peg Roy; Alex Jacobs; Ruth Woodward; Martha and Steve Millard; Pat and Brenda Mothersell; Eleanor Sweeney; Neal Burdick; Béatrice Machet and William Franke; Sarah Iselin and Frank Parman of Oklahoma; Joe Bruchac; Stephanie Sellers; Lisa Tatonetti; my editors Chris Shaw and Amanda Lanne-Camilli; Kathleen Masterson; Donald McNutt; Vic DeGhett and Stephanie Coyne-DeGhett and Torie Rose DeGhett; Jan Robbins; Nancy and John Berbrich; Terry Tiernan; Holly Chambers; Alan Steinberg; Jim Donahue; John Youngblood; Ethan Shantie; Carter Jones, Kayla (Riley) and Alex French; Jimmie Dixon; Kevin Bertolero; Jeanette Godreau; all of my students, all of my listeners, all of my readers . . . thank you for being there.

one

Boyhood

Growing up is hard to do. Growing up Indian in the United States is very hard to do. Growing up a half-blood is painful. Growing up a writer/poet is almost impossible. Filling in the blanks between these various aspects of life may prove to be even more difficult: first locating the puzzle, then the pieces, and discovering the blank spots for the pieces to fit into the jigsaw. The when, why, and wherefore. Plus the possible embarrassments to you and yours. Going from A to whatever alphabet letter you stop on can cause pain and anger to rise up from not only your own being but the downright hostile motives of those who become adjuncts to you, the subject. Where do you begin, end? What do you reveal, eliminate, emphasize, discreetly lighten up on? I believe it was Jean-Jacques Rousseau who said that the writer always must seek for truth, and I agree, but is this possible in the composition of an autobiographical piece? Should the truth be abandoned for sincerity? Truth may have nothing whatsoever to do with the vividness of memory, its sparkle or dulled edge.

Years *do* dull the edge, to say nothing of all that comes with them. Nothing remains rapier sharp. Who remembers what he had for breakfast yesterday, the tie worn Monday, why you played the ace of spades when you knew who had the queen of spades in the game of hearts? Can memory be trusted to be utterly truthful? Is truth equal with fact? The scientist deals with facts, the poet with beauty, and is there truth in beauty? Let us ignore John Keats's answer for the moment. Beauty is in the eye of the beholder. If that is true, then is truth in the eye of the speaker who is a beholder as well? And is the truth of the Mohawk the same as the truth of the Hopi?

All tribal mores deal with the concept of truth. It was wrong to lie to your own people, chief, village, but it was near-heroic to lie to the white invader of your homeland. And what is the truth of Christianity? There are more sects nearly each day. Should we live by the Bible, the sword, the word of Jesus Christ, Emerson's Over-Soul, Jung's collective unconscious or the echoes of time itself? Perhaps we merely count the rings of a virgin pine and claim these rings to be the absolute, the truth of humanity and all life around us. But, what of the tree's memory? Does it fade after the first one hundred years? Can it be factual? So much depends on a red wheelbarrow. Famines may have passed this pine, insects, snows, or lack of snows. Can the circles be trusted? The tree too has a memory that may fill it from season to season. I would as soon trust last night's dream or nightmare. It rises from the soul, the being, the essence, the fears and joys, the subconscious, through a motif of symbolic images. William Carlos Williams was right: "This is just to say . . ."

And that is what I have done. I have eaten the plums "so cold and so sweet." I remember most things, and yes, I do remember what I had for breakfast yesterday (a toasted roll with blackberry jam and the ever-present mug of black coffee). Memory is fairly sound; beauty is wished for; truth is of the utmost in this presentation, but only as far as memory allows. The art of dodging, I can master that sport.

And, I think, attempt to recall the angry rains. I wasn't always pampered. No, not at all.

What am I doing here?

Biting through skin to the pulp of flesh . . . my mother said I was born on the hottest day of any August she could remember. It was a dark night. She could not tell me the exact hour. Did pain prohibit her memory from functioning correctly, truthfully, or was she hiding something? My sisters, Agnes and Mary, were both autumn births . . . delivery is easier on cooler days, or nights. Perhaps it is for this reason that they received a bit more understanding from my mother than I was fortunate to know. I do not believe it was because they shared a gender that I did not. My mother, although she complained of the cold and hated winter, also always hated the heat of summer. I felt she blamed me for this heat . . . having been born on the hottest August night she could remember. It is possible through records to check the exact temperature that night—August 16, 1929—but, frankly, I don't care to. Some biographical background concerning my mother: she was born a farm girl in the township of Cape Vincent, New York, a few miles from the St. Lawrence River. The family Bible, still in the possession of her sister, my aunt Jennie Sanford, claims my grandfather to be descended from Robert Herrick, the English poet. Her father's people, the Herricks and the Clarks, were in northern New York from the early 1800s onward. She was also a descendent of the Parkers; General Ely S. Parker is specified, if memory serves. Her mother, Leona, was both a Parker and an Oatman. She was born in Adams Center, New York, and was an eighth Seneca. My mother attended the stereotypical one-room schoolhouse, and she later would say that it was red as well. Exactly how far she went in school is debatable. From her knowledge of books, and so forth, I would guess not further than what they used to call "the Sixth Book," a fairly rudimentary education, if also more than most of her peers would likely have received. Not necessarily a strong religious woman, she had been baptized a Baptist, though I never can remember her reading or toting a copy of the "good book." Yet she read most of her life: mainly women's magazines and, later, biographies of the rich and famous. She had no artistic abilities of which I was ever aware, with the exception of crocheting. The house was choked by doilies. Almost to the day she died, she gave us presents of doilies for Christmas and birthdays. I have some still.

She left the farm, as the other six sisters needed to do, and, also like the others, became a scullery maid for the rich in Watertown, New York. From photos I gather she was a pretty girl, small and thin, but stylish . . . at least as stylish as her income would allow. She married young, and bore her first child, my sister Agnes, young. Although no one has ever convinced me she did not love my biological father, I can't help but believe she thought always she had made a mistake in marrying and bearing children so young, but maybe that's Addie Bundren's complaint ringing in my ears, not my mother's. I think my mother would have been much happier playing our childish games with us than making supper for us. She never seemed to take much pride in her cooking, nor was she a really fine cook. Her pastry was good, but as to her roast . . . well, perhaps I should not comment. My parents separated when I was nine years old. It was painful for all concerned. I went with her by choice . . . one of the many bad choices I have made in my life. She was not a good teacher . . . but more on this later. I think this marriage could have been saved had either of my parents considered a counselor. My father was stubborn and my mother wispy, neither of which inclined them toward that course.

Andrew Anthony Kenny was born in 1900 on a farm outside a small Canadian village in the province of Ontario. His father, Maurice—pronounced like Morris—was not only Irish, but it was jokingly said that he was born on the boat while crossing the Atlantic. My grandmother was an Indian woman, Mohawk. I know little of her except that she was a West. She died young, having birthed three children, the same as my mother . . . two older girls and one son, my father. I don't recall exactly how old my father was at his mother's death, but he was still a young lad. His father married a second time, an Irishwoman, which meant that there was as much Irish nationalism as there was Indianism in my father's rearing. His cousins have always taken pride in the fact that relatives still live and breathe in Ireland, and when I was younger they supported the idea that I go and make my visit . . . which I have resisted all my life for varying reasons. As I grew into adolescence, my father began talking more and more to me about his own boyhood, and more frequently told stories concerning his mother. He never ignored his Irish father, though, and spoke many times of relatives still living in Ireland. I even remember once he said that at school, if a teacher asked what my nationality was, I was to tell them that I was Irish and English . . . nothing more. He said it would make for "a better understanding."

He had only two years of schooling, what he called "the Second Book," but what most, then and now, would call the second grade. He could—with hesitation—read and write. He was a hard worker, industrious, and serious, not to mention aggressive and competitive . . . he believed deeply in both his ability and his obligation to be a self-made man. When he died in 1957 he was either the proprietor or the lessee of three gas stations and a restaurant. He was continuously ill the last five years of his life, but this illness did not hinder him from building a new home, in which he lived only one year.

My dad was reckless as a youth. He had constant conflicts with his father and buried his head in his stepmother's bosom when his two older sisters were not binding his wounds. He was allowed to drive the horse and buggy . . . I cannot believe it was a surrey . . . to the church euchre game, but if he overstayed his father's rule by a minute, Maurice would be there at the church stable to take the horse and buggy home, forcing my father to walk the many miles late on a winter's cold night.

My father enjoyed telling stories, especially when lecturing me about smoking cigarettes, recounting how he burned his father's hay barn down. He'd laugh and tell how he smoked one day, rolling his tobacco in some form of paper . . . possibly leaves . . . lit up, took a drag or two, and fell promptly asleep, having stayed out late the night before at the church dance. That was one occasion on which his father came to collect the horse and buggy. Naturally, in his doze, he dropped the lighted cigarette. The hay caught afire, and before long he was trying to stamp out the blazing furnace of the barn. Sometimes he would say that he stayed at the farm only long enough to receive the thrashing of his life. Other times he said he just hightailed it off the place as fast as his fourteen-year-old legs would carry him. The family down the road gave him sanctuary, and then he took off for the States, directly to Watertown where he first stayed with his aunt Libby. Having the good luck of landing a job, he also found a room on State Street in the home of one old lady, a Mrs. Collins, who mothered him like a blood son. He loved this lady greatly. She passed on before I had opportunity of knowing her. He would never admit it, but I believe his smoking and causing the barn to burn to the rocky ground was an act of wish-fulfillment; subconsciously he not only wanted to take some revenge on his father, but he also was looking for an escape hatch. He hated farming, as did my mother. He was able to groom out the farmer in his character and style rather quickly.

He took to city life . . . Watertown's population was then about thirty thousand, a sprawling metropolis for the time and for the region. He never spoke about it, but I can easily visualize him at pool halls and in the bars, which were still called "buckets of blood" due to the vicious fights that broke out nightly. A cousin was in the position to obtain a job for my dad. His was a most aqueous labor: he became the water boy on the gang of the city of Watertown's Water Department. His job was to carry the water bucket to the workers, to men who were digging new lines. He stayed at the waterworks for many years and by the time he left, he had risen to foreman, the third most important position within that department. As foreman, he had been in a position to hire and fire the work-gangs that did minor, occasional jobs. He hired many immigrant Italians who could not speak much, if any, English but were married to marvelous cooks, and my family and I often partook of rich pastas and still richer red "dago" wine that were prepared for us as tokens of gratitude.

My father also hired many Native men who had come down from the Kahnawake Mohawk community near Montreal or from Akwesasne, a Mohawk community on the St. Lawrence that straddles the U.S.-Canadian border. These Native men who came to Watertown seeking work with their wives and children naturally needed homes. My father was in the position to help, and he did. He was always a just and generous man, though there were times during my adolescence when I questioned his ethics. He became political, and it was not beneath him to ask small favors of elected officials with a quart of bourbon in his hands. The city owned several houses, and for reasons I cannot fathom, these houses came under the jurisdiction of the Water Department. Of course, my father saw that the Natives were given the houses. Rent in those days was something like five dollars a month.

Though he helped get several Native families settled in housing near the house in which my family lived, my father cautioned me not to play with the children. He gave no reason. His word was law, though I was often discovered breaking that law. As a small child my father rarely spoke of his Indian heritage because of the stigma. It was not a time to shout, "Hey, I'm an Indian" in North America, let alone in either southern Ontario or northern New York. He would tell stories or sing songs without identifying the source. He told the stories as though he had just simply used his imagination and had at that precise moment invented the tale or the song. Yet he was teaching, and he meant to teach. He intended that I would learn these stories, though I'm not sure he anticipated my using the tales years later in poems that I would write. I don't think he had any idea that I would become a writer. It wasn't until I entered high school that

I really showed much artistic interest. I painted, but not well. I sang, but shyly. I wrote many poems and stories, but this writing showed little talent to those around me who judged such things. I did write many, many letters to the editor of the *Watertown Daily Times*. In high school I was busy riding horses, working for my father, attending weekend teenage dances at the school or YMCA, camping and swimming.

My father was a hunter, a fisherman, an outdoor man. I most always went along on his fishing trips, but I rarely got to go hunting with him. That was probably due to interference by my mother. She was afraid of guns. She hated cleaning the rabbits or pheasants he would bring home in his game bag. She also hated cleaning the fish he brought home on the string, but complied reluctantly. He talked hunting with me. Talked about his hound dogs. The smells of his rifles, his hunting boots, and his outerwear were always in the house. I always knew that his guns were stored in a closet in my parents' bedroom. It was never locked. I had access to it, but his teachings were strong, and I never had the desire to take the guns out of the closet and play with them. He did ask me to help clean and oil the guns from time to time. And he would tell hunting stories, though they were not tall tales about how the largest rabbit in the woods got away, or how the bear pulled the gun out of his hands and whacked him across the head with it. He never hunted bears. He never shot a bear. He held a distinct aversion for bears. But no . . . no, no, no . . . that is not the correct word; he had not an aversion, but a reverence for bears, who I gradually came to know and to understand as Bear through his perspective.

Bear is a mighty animal, not merely for physical strength, but mighty in tradition, medicine. Bear was a relative: you do not kill or eat your brother, nor walk on his back. Bear is a mystery, spirit, legend; it is the unknown, it is the poetic. Perhaps not as noble a beast as Wolf, Bear is still not without nobility in the animal world, which includes the human species. Bear is the enigma of the woods—not of the wilderness, because there is no such thing as wilderness. The wild is in the human spirit and human mind, and Bear is a wildness beyond humanity. When bears are extinct, then the woods are forever gone. Then the darkness, the shadows, the voices, the healing powers, the medicines of the woods will be lost into the past, the time of the past. Culture will be doomed. Bear's flesh should never be eaten, nor should his spirit be desecrated by making bearskins into a wall decoration or a rug before a fireplace. To wear a robe about one's shoulders made of a bear found dead on the forest floor of natural causes is and will be a compliment, an honor to Bear, but to step on his back with dirty boots is an abominable idea. Bear is the last freedom. His extinction would be the most horrible of tragedies. Bear is the symbol of humanism, not the untamed or conquerable wilderness.

Wolf, though he is in great jeopardy from the foolishness of Man, has at least some semblance of immortality in that he is the grandfather of coyote and of the common domesticated house or lap dog. He will continue to be hunted and slaughtered because Man hates him and fears his fangs, and because historically he has competed with Man for sustenance, food. I believe there is a gene in the American/European that insists upon ridding the world of Wolf. Yet humans can learn how to live from Wolf, how to live with one another without genocidal wars caused by religions and overbreeding.

My father taught respect for Bear and Wolf, but he also taught respect for wild iris, or blue flag, for trillium and cattail. He taught respect for corn, berries, water, winds. He knew their strengths. The wild iris renews the premise and promise of beauty and poetry, the song that abounds around us, that circles our natures and is a reminder of that great green ceremony of which the Lakota holy man Black Elk spoke so graciously and wisely: the green ceremony of everyday is to lift the head from the pillow and see the beauties and gifts of the day, and to be thankful.

My father also had many artistic bents, but realized none except song. He loved to sing, particularly Friday nights when a beer or four encouraged the voice:

> If I had the wings of a turtle / over these prison walls I would fly.

It was impossible to convince him turtles did not have wings. He was either thinking of the turtledove, or he remembered something his biological mother had told him as a small child: that she was a member of the turtle clan. I believe those early stories stuck and manifested in him as the turtle flying over the prison walls, even if it was originally a wished-for angel that did the flying in that old folk song.

As I said, he was a good storyteller and was also an excellent listener, except when we children were in trouble and attempted to explain a way out of it to him. Then his ears were closed. He knew the reasons better than we did, and he acted upon them. Even then, he was not mean. He was usually considerate, generous, and warm. My grandfather was a "mean" man. My aunt Julia, my dad's sister, said Maurice was *mean* in an Irish fashion. My father was never a mean man, though he had a most outrageous temper, as on occasion he would prove through his actions. More often than not, though, he was the lamb; he had a soft smile, a twinkle in the eye, and a generous manner . . . usually. He rarely beat us, again something handed down from his Mohawk mother. Indians do not beat their children. They teach bad from good by example.

I did receive one terrifying beating from him, and my sister, Mary, got a vicious one from him when he was drunk. Agnes, his favorite, was never touched. He slapped my mother several times during arguments. She was a nagger. She had been given warnings. But he slapped her regardless. Thinking back now I have the tendency to think that she might have deserved the slaps. But using my head, my reasoning, I remind myself, no, she did not. No woman deserves to be brutalized. He was an extremely strong man: short, heavy, stocky, far stronger than the pitiful little creature my mother was . . . never weighing more than ninety pounds. No man is ever right in striking, let alone beating, a woman. He was wrong. I remember once he hit her, and I, a mere piddle of a runt, picked up a broom and tried to defend her womanhood and physical weakness. He held it against me all his life.

Another example of his anger came out one Christmas, as he was dressing the tree he had gone to the woods to chop. He enjoyed celebrating holidays, indeed ceremonies of all kinds, with the exceptions of birthdays, never accepting the fact that the celebrant should receive a gift for merely having been born. He observed this rite reluctantly. In those days, the 1930s, electric Christmas lights were not the reliably mass-produced perfection they are now. They had, as it is often said, a mind of their own, and the bulbs on the wire frequently found the inclination to light up and spread the colored cheer around the living room at unexpected times. He had the wires strung out straight as a toothpick . . . the colored bulbs all screwed into the tiny sockets, male into female, and plugged the string into the electrical socket. Nothing happened. Not a single spark, not a single blue, red or green, or yellow, or white flashed against the wall where he sat puttering with the set. He worked for at least half an hour. Nothing. No color. No contact. My sisters and I sat near, delighting in the knowledge of the upcoming festivities, both the presents we'd receive and the edible goodies we would push into our young tummies: the homemade taffy my dad had made; the maple walnut fudge my mother's kid sister, Aunt Frances, had whipped up; the roast duck my father had shot and which my mother was cooking in the woodstove; the oranges we were given only on Christmas; the mincemeat pie; the cranberry sauce; the chocolate cake my grandmother Herrick had made and the ribbon candy Aunt Jennie brought one evening before. We knew exactly where my mother had hidden the gifts that would be attributed to Santa's delivery on the night before Christmas. We had watched her buy the wool stockings, the shirts, and the sweaters, clothes we would desperately need to cross the cold northern winters but which, in our hearts, we detested. We hoped she had not forgotten a toy or two, perhaps at least some books. Happiness glowed around the kitchen woodstove.

My mother puttered about, slicing fruit for an applejack pudding; Aunt Frances was preening, applying makeup for her date later that evening; my sisters and I were crumpled in expectation and delight, frozen in anticipation of the coming act of celebration and joy. My father mumbled. Then he cursed. Took *the* name in vain. Called out something impertinent to my mother, like . . . I told you to buy these at Sears. He never tired of complaining that my mother was a spendthrift, that she always wasted rather than conserved. For example, she bought packaged butter, rather than a less costly pound from the grocer's tub. Suddenly, he rose from the straight chair, numerous strands of electric lights entwined around his body, arms, and legs, whirling the loose wires over his head as if a lasso. He stomped out of the living room and, returned with the tree now tangled in the wire, went to the cellar door, and upon opening it, threw tree and wires and himself as one down the stairs. We all laughed . . . all but our mother. She knew better. She understood the consequences of our laughing in his face at his foolishness and at his failure. In a few moments he crawled sheepishly up the stairs. We continued to laugh. Taking his coat and the hat that he nearly always wore, he went to the kitchen door, pronouncing as he strode through that there would be no Christmas this year in the Kenny household, nor the next, nor the next. He kept his word . . . at least for the following year. That year, we ate hamburgers, which my sister Agnes cooked. My father and mother were not there. Later Agnes said they had gone to the bar on Christmas Eve, were drunk, and had not come home.

I suppose that this outrage and my father's temper helps explain why Christmas has never been important to me. First, the kitchen scene was to leave an indelible mark on my mind. This is a Christian holiday feted with pagan trappings . . . the tree, the lights. I have nothing against celebrating the birth of Jesus Christ. I honor Him, pay respect to His codes, words. Christmas can be and should be a spiritual day, the same as Gandhi's birthday, or Martin Luther King Jr.'s and, yes, Crazy Horse's, or the Iroquois Peacemaker's . . . that is, if we knew his day of birth. Such spiritual celebration need not stem from Christian reality. I am not a Christian but a pagan. I was baptized a Roman Catholic but left those teachings behind at a very early age. I think it was in the third grade when I announced to the nun, my teacher, that I thought human beings were descended from monkeys. She had no use for Darwinian thought. I think right then was the first—though not the last—time that I was excommunicated from the church. Spirituality, spirit, religion, faith starts in the human heart, not as a catechism nor a black book that can serve many needs by those seeking rational approval for wrong deeds.

Few high school lads have solid relationships with their fathers. I was no different from any other. I believed my father to be obsessively conventional, tough, restrictive. Thinking back now, I see that he wasn't as tough as I then believed. He was permissive with the exception that I was to rise early in the morning, and when not in school, I had to work in either his gas station or his restaurant. This he did demand of me. He was teaching a work ethic, trying to give me a business sense, a saving-for-a-rainy-day attitude, and he prompted or persuaded me to think in terms of a business major. What I did in my spare time, such as writing or painting, or even singing, well, that could be the reward for being smartly industrious and a good businessman. My father was no different from most fathers. His life had been hard, with a fraction of an education, and he wanted to ensure that mine would be easier. I, of course, did not think that way, but the opposite. My philosophy was, "Let the future take care of the future. It would in all likelihood happen anyway."

I have no doubt whatsoever that the greatest influence on my life, actions, and thinking was exerted by my father. He encouraged me in all ways, and not only to accumulate goods and monies, but to stop, even with one foot inside the counting house, and to observe the minute things of life: the ant crawling across the cabbage leaf, the tremolo of the loon, the birth of the blossom, the wheeling of the hawk in the sky, the sweet, good smell of the wild strawberry laden with mystery in the sun-drenched field or along the shady path. He was a hunter of flesh, and I became the hunter of words, but he was the first teacher. He taught me how to prepare the gun, how to keep it in good shape, how to fire, and what to fire it upon. How different a man, a human, I would be had my father been any other than who he was! If I write poems or short stories, and if I write them well, it is to show him . . . perhaps to prove to him . . . that I have become a bad business person who spends no time at all in the counting house. Rather, I have become a hunter and bring home to the door the trophies of a hunter of words, of language.

two

Life in the North

Childhood was not all celebration and lazy summer days, cool swims in the lake, picking sweet berries in fields or woods. My parents argued a great deal; there were arguments in my Aunt Jennie's house, though those usually happened in the bedroom, not in the kitchen in front of the children. If we went visiting, it was in the winter, on weekends, or to funerals or marriages. It was more often to my father's people across the St. Lawrence in Canada, to the homes of my aunts, Julia and Cecily, or to the farm belonging to Uncle Eugene, his half-brother. My grandmother Herrick was not honey-natured. I think she did not like children, despite having had seven daughters and one son who died in infancy. We thought she was just old-fashioned, but later I decided she was an embittered aging lady who had no real home of her own and visited her married daughters' homes in relays of three months. When she was at my father's house, she constantly found fault with my sisters and me, and bided the afternoon until my father returned home for supper and she could report our mischievousness . . . or at least what she thought was our badness. He paid little attention to her complaints, despite their chronic recurrence.

As a youngster, I spent most of my summers on a farm on Fox Creek Road, a few miles from Cape Vincent. There was fun even on the farm, though it was often mixed in with toil and occasional torment. I had to rise early and milk cows. Often, and to my shame, my aunt Ruth would hold me down while my uncle Frank, Jennie's husband, would squirt the hot milk from the cow's teat directly into my mouth. It hung dry, sticky, and foul-smelling. It seemed it never left my skin or my clothes. They laughed at my embarrassment. Some of my fun came from picking berries: the strawberries in the hot fields, the hickory nuts in the fall. Joy also came from the winter sleigh rides with hot bread and sweet jam, or from the applejack that Aunt Jennie made for us with pleasure, placing cups of hot chocolate beside the plate of pie still steaming from the oven. I had to help dig a water well once, and that hurt my sensibilities, but now these many years later I fully realize Uncle Frank was teaching a sense of work ethic and responsibility. It was for my own good. Even though the dust set off my hay fever, haymaking was fun, . . . the cutting, gathering, storing off in the mounds. Aunt Jennie always made buckets of ginger beer, which I could not drink because she made it with a fresh egg. My serious egg allergy would not allow me to partake of the frothy liquid that filled the pail she would bring out to us. Instead, I would serve it to the men haying the fields and, later on, to the thrashers.

In the summer, Uncle Frank would take us to the beach for watermelon picnics after Sunday chores were finished. During the week he would take us into town, Three Mile Bay, a village of only a few hundred; while he was conducting his business, we could enter the huge store there and buy candies. The store was marvelous, filled with a child's treasures: candies, pretty ribbons, shoestrings, yo-yos, paper and pencil and small workbooks, stationery, and funny fishhooks. It also was well stocked with good things that adults enjoyed, like bricks of cheddar cheese, smoked fish, and tropical fruits like bananas and oranges, which were difficult to find in the North Country in those days. Sometimes Uncle Frank would leave us sitting for hours in his old Chevrolet. When he returned he always had a gift . . . perhaps a bag of pretzels . . . and he always had huge smiles, grins that spread from ear to ear. His face was often flushed, his eyes utterly alive, and his breath smelling of a strange nutty odor: beer, we would later find out.

We arrived back at the farm . . . sometimes well after the accustomed supper hour . . . Aunt Jennie would be in the master bedroom down the hall from the dining room and across the hall from the formal parlor. Grandma Herrick would be arguing in the kitchen with Aunt Ruth. Periodically, Aunt Ruth would come out to shush our whispers. We could hear arguments going on behind two sets of doors. We were desperately trying to eavesdrop on these fights. Usually Aunt Jennie would not come out of the room until the words ceased hurtling back and forth. Uncle Frank would come out, having lost the flush to his countenance, and turn his attention to the evening chores.

In the early years, Grandpa Kenny was a real teaser. He thoroughly enjoyed holding an Indian nickel before my eyes, and as I reached for it, he would snatch it away. This game seemed to go on forever and I was never allowed to claim the coin. The other game I played was with Uncle Jim. Not only was he a greater tease than my grandfather, he sparkled when he teased. He always told me I could take a horse home when we visited with him and I always believed him. My mother constantly warned him that he would need to deal with me when the hour of our departure back to the States arrived. After all, I could see no reason why we couldn't just tie the horse to the car and let it trot behind us . . . yes, right onto the ferry or across the long bridge that was built at Wellesley Island before the Second World War, while Franklin Roosevelt was president.

I always loved horses and my Uncle Jim's regular teasing kept them in my mind's sight, if not my actual possession. My Uncle Frank had this one horse on his place. I didn't know it at the time, but this horse, due to long years of toil, was blind and had been put out to pasture. I tried desperately to mount this black animal and ride off into the windy fields, but I could never stand him still long enough to mount his bare back. Instead, I would try to ride the calves in the barnyard. That didn't work well either. One morning before going off to pick berries, I noticed the old horse was standing below a wild plum tree. Nearby was a pile of rocks and one large boulder, upon which he butted his rear end. I crept stealthily across the field. He did not smell me because the winds were blowing gently from the other way. I climbed the granite boulder. I had my hands onto his thick mane before he scented my flesh. I was up, on, and away . . . but not for long! In mere seconds, he tossed me into a barbed-wire fence. I have carried the scar on my left calf ever since.

All my relatives on both sides of the family really seemed to get a huge charge from taunting me. I've yet to figure out why. Was it because I was short and thin? Was it because I had bad allergies? Was it because I was a boy who lived with two sisters in a small city while they lived in rural areas? Was it because my cousins were all older and wiser than I and had formed an alliance with my two older sisters, who were already sovereign over me at home? My sisters easily won the games we played in the tomato patch, throwing rotten fruits at each other as if they were snowballs. They also silently witnessed my punishment for being covered with streaming tomato juice, seeds in my hair and skins hanging from my ears, when I came back to the house. I have never liked a single one of my numerous cousins. Never! Not one. I was the enemy to them. This was true of both sides of the family. When I turned five, my father bought me my first tricycle. In a fit of jealousy, my cousin Morris, who was two years older than I, carried my tricycle onto the railroad tracks. The train was charging down the rails and, naturally, my tricycle was smashed. When my father came home from work, he spanked me. Never again did I have a tricycle, though when I was in my early teens he did buy me a Sears Roebuck Elgin bike for my birthday. I think he made me clean out the garage before I received the gift, though. As I said before, he did not believe in being celebrated simply for having been born.

I remember iris springs, chicory summers, maple-leaf falls, and snowdrift winters. I remember the chicory summers best, perhaps. The skies were blue as my strange eyes, the eyes that always get questioned wherever I go. An Okanagan woman once asked me during lunch if all my family had blue eyes, and I told her the story of how a strange man in Saranac Lake one day stopped me on the street and asked if I was Maurice Kenny, the Mohawk poet. Naturally, my reply was "yes." "Where did you get those blue eyes?" he asked. "You know," I said, "that's exactly what my father asked my mother. You know what she answered? She told him, 'It's none of your business.'" The world does not seem to want to accept the blood quantum that flows in my veins. I'm always being questioned. My work is saturated with poems dealing with this theme. What is an Indian . . . blood, heart, spirit, color?

I would spend mornings along the brown river shores with my father. Together, we would be fishing or netting the minnows. Later, he would sell to the fishermen who were touring from Utica or Syracuse. He made money. These mornings were special. It was time spent with a man I was attempting to understand and to love, and from whom I also needed love. It was a time in which he could speak and bring home values to me. As a young child, I could still weigh and eventually accept these things; as I grew into adolescence, though, this became increasingly unlikely. No teenager believes their parent; all parents are wrong. Parents do not understand boys' or girls' problems; after all, *they* never had the same experiences. I spoke little in return to my father on those iris mornings by the river. I was shy and afraid. Some awe possessed me, making me terrified of confessing my true thoughts and feelings to him . . . much to my regret now, of course. It is always too late. He had much to teach. He did not have the answers to many of my questions simply because there are no answers to some of our questions. He taught me to love the river, the waters, the fish, the wild grass weaving in the current, even the rocks on the river bottom, and the flowers, iris, and pickerel. He taught me to enjoy the sun and to sit calmly and quietly, contemplating this free beauty. This lyric that nature and the Creator so bountifully has loaned to us all.

One of the things that I kept from my father was an experience I suffered one summer at Aunt Jennie's farm. An older man of my parents' age lived down the road on another farm. My mother had attended the red schoolhouse with him and knew him all her life. There were always cold whispers, giving my sisters and I the impression that he was a dirty old man and that the girls should stay away from him. My aunts, Jennie and Ruth, always told us to come away whenever he approached us, whether it was on the road, in the yard, or certainly in the field. My beagle hound, Happy, was with me at the farm that summer. He had a tendency to run away at the first sniff of a rabbit. One day, he did just that and Aunt Jennie commanded that I find him, bring him home, and tie him up. I followed through my grandfather's abandoned apple orchard . . . moldering in time. Uncle Frank cared little about his husbandry duties to the fruit trees, and so the apples were small and wormy. Even the small grape arbor at the side of the orchard was ignored. Only one apple tree behind the house shed was ever respected, a translucent tree in which my grandfather took particular interest. This tree was pruned, and the apples were used in many delicious ways on the supper table. I followed Happy through the neglected orchard and across a lot where Uncle Frank's pigsty stood. The odor was outrageous. As I neared, the pigs grunted, hoping I had slop or whey for them. Further on, I ambled into a kind of scrub-brush jungle where there were cedars, crabapple trees. It was here I found Happy being held by the man who lived down the road. He had him on a rope. I don't recall our conversation, other than him asking if I wanted to play a little game before I took the hound home. As a kid, I said yes. I liked games. All kids do. He said he had to tie me to the maple tree nearby and would show me how the game was played. In utter innocence, I smiled, laughed, and complied with his instructions. He tied me to the trunk around my waist above the belt line, with my hands to each side. I watched him drool, stand back, and then approach me. He unbuttoned my pants, allowed them to fall, then pulled down my shorts and stooped in front of me. In all honesty, it did feel good. But shame covered me completely. I had sinned. I knew *somehow* I had sinned or given this man the right to sin upon me. Therefore I was guilty as he was of the sin. Before he released me from the ropes, he said I must promise never to tell, not Uncle Frank, my father, or anyone. I promised, and he released me from the binds.

That man followed my steps through adolescence: he would follow me down the street; he called me out of class during school hours; he would beg me to sit in his car when school was out; he offered to drive me home. It was impossible to get rid of him, but it was also impossible to tell my father, who probably would have shot the man on sight. I never have told anyone until writing these words down and I'm *still* in fear that my father . . . dead these long years . . . is listening to my words and oiling up his deer rifle. Needless to say, this experience, frightening and shameful as it was, has haunted my life. It taught me to be wary and never trust an adult man. The iris springs and the chicory summers were spoiled. A wild thing had been bruised; a wildflower had been crushed . . . and would be again in summers and winters to come.

Childhood had its pleasure and pain . . . that I shall not deny. And looking back, I probably see it more golden-hued than it truly was. There were many family problems of which I was only half aware, in which I was only slightly interested, or barely understood, even if I *was* aware of and interested in them. They were family rows. I didn't quite understand death or birth. Marriage was an enigma. I did not understand why my mother did not like to be near water when her belly was sometimes huge and round . . . for reasons that I also could not fathom, in part because they were not told to me. My father bought an old summer cabin in Chaumont Bay on Lake Ontario. She fought because she did not want to go there even though my dad, my sisters, and I were so fond of it. I figured it was because he would go back to the city for work all week and was there only from Friday nights to Monday mornings. She was lonely in her weekly abandonment and did not really enjoy our company. It was years later when Agnes told me that my father had made her pregnant and that she had miscarried when she was near the lake waters. Perhaps she had a fear of him tossing her out of the fishing rowboat. He did this to me once, far out on the lake, when he attempted to teach me how to swim back to shore. Most of the time, though, she was in her element being near the water. She fished avidly, especially for bullheads (sometimes known as catfish), and didn't even squirm when she cleaned the slimy, scaly creatures before cooking them. I have always hated bullheads and refuse to eat them when served. We loved the cottage/cabin. We loved the water, the rocky shore, the picnic up at the Point, and the deep woods across the mud road. We wandered there picking hickory nuts off the ground, scampering, and searching for guinea pigs or baby rabbits. Of course, we got into trouble when we brought them back to the kitchen and my mother screamed. We fought Labor Day's arrival and having to go back to school with the nuns.

For the first six years of my schooling I was forced to study with the sisters of Saint Joseph. It was hell at Holy Family School. It was not really a boarding school, but to me it had all the earmarks of one. Perhaps my sisters did not need to go through what I had to with the nuns. Mary simply did her work and asked for nothing. Consequently, other than in Latin, she had few problems and managed to emerge fairly happy and unscathed, even after attending the convent high school. Agnes adored the school and the nuns. In today's parlance, Agnes would be a brownnoser. She had few problems with the nuns and wept broadly when she graduated from the convent high school. I shall never forget my sisters in their black uniforms with white round collars. Every morning they fought over their uniforms. The uniforms were costly and several were needed. Yet now, it seems like they never had a clean uniform in which to attend school. They did, but still complained bitterly. My father insisted that their graduation from that high school signified an education equivalent to college. This was not true, although they did come out with some polish, some sense, and some Latin and French. They also lost their northern New York accents and could even sing pretty well, especially Agnes, who maintained a lovely voice throughout her life.

I, however, could not wait to get out from under the nuns' odd combination of black skirts and checkered aprons. My oldest and strongest memories of the nuns involve only pain, misery, and hate. Holy Family had been donated to the church by a very wealthy family whose name I don't believe I ever heard. It consisted of two colored buildings: gray for the grammar school and brick red for the junior high school. I never attended school in the red building, which housed the mother superior's office, although, I visited it often . . . and *not* for a cup of tea or compliments. Behind the gray building was a marvelous formal French garden, through which we were allowed to stroll during recess. "BUT DO NOT TOUCH THE FLOWERS!" If you picked one, whether intentionally or by mistake, you were as good as dead. To the right of the garden was a swimming pool. Most of the time, it was empty, which made it another dangerous place. Beyond the pool was a high stone fence, which enclosed a lot. Here, they forced us to play baseball. It was in this lot that I learned to hate baseball . . . and I still do to this very day. I always mumbled that I was sick and dizzy and could not swing the bat, run, or catch; sometimes that got me out of playing, but often it did not. I remember the lot was ringed with a bed of yellow flowers. Being spring, they were probably dandelions. I do not hold my pain against those wildflowers.

Untouchable flowers and compulsory athletics were not the worst of it, though. In third grade we were taught scriptwriting. I never really learned it with any precision or beauty. There was hell to pay if, when dunking the wood pen and point into the inkwell, you should spatter the ink on the braids of the girl sitting in front of you, or stain your shirt or your fingers with it. You were taken downstairs to the boys' room in the basement and made to stand on a wide, high wood platform before an enormous sink. The sink seemed nearly as huge as the empty swimming pool out by the garden. There you were roughly washed and scrubbed clean until not a trace of ink was left. It was also at this sink where a goodly sister would toothcomb your head, looking for lice. And should you have one . . . lo and behold, you were in serious trouble. How *dare* your mother allow you to come to school with lice? Never mind that our mothers were often the culprits, the first hosts of the lice. My mother particularly enjoyed going to J. J. Newberry's or Woolworth's to try on hats, and as a result, she would bring lice home to us. Once, when I gossiped about my poor mother's unwitting penchant for lousy hats, the nun insisted I was lying and washed my puckered mouth out with Fels-Naptha soap. It was not especially tasty, and not really a sweet mouthwash. All the students had their mouths washed out with that vile soap, more usually used for cleaning and curing poison ivy infection. It was used if anything near a curse word would be uttered, or if a word of Mohawk passed our lips. I can still taste that soap to this moment. When washing my face, I always do it with a washcloth so that my lips and mouth are not contaminated by any soap.

The most excruciating pain we felt from those sisters of Saint Joseph, though, was when we were again led down to the boys' room near the wood platform in the basement of the gray building. We filed into this dungeon, with one lightbulb dangling from the ceiling, to find a long low trough against the wall. A nun stood at the far end with a pointer stick at the ready in her hand. If a urinating boy should spray the wall above the trough, the thin pointer would come quickly down onto his penis. Believe me it hurt. Why did they hate the penis so greatly? Again, this was something I did not dare take home to my parents, especially when no word pertaining to sex was ever mentioned in my father's house. I never once saw my father or mother naked. Only once did I even witness my father urinate, and that was at the river's shore while fishing one morning. The sisters of Saint Joseph did a lot of damage to the boys. I have no idea what they might have accomplished with the girls. They were brutal and for the most part I found them to be insensitive to the needs of the children. Far from being concerned for the poor, they even castigated you if your parents did not have money and could not contribute to the church with either cash or food. I have no idea if my father complied. We were not poverty-stricken. It was the Depression, but my father always had a new Chevy. He bought the lakeshore cabin and we had warm clothes and good food, though much of it was wild game, fish, deer, rabbit, or pheasant.

There was one nun whom I liked. Her name was Sister Dorothea and she was beautiful to behold. Her face was the color of a very light honey and it shone under the light as if she were oiled. She was my fifth-grade teacher. She was also the music teacher and the conductor of the chorus. I might have loved her if it had not been for the horrible experiences I'd had with the other nuns at Holy Family School. She discovered my voice and had me sing. In fact, on one Christmas Eve in the church I sang "Silent Night" alone. I was always terrified while in that church . . . the statues and icons put me off considerably. Were they real? At the left side of the church was the hanging cross of Christ's crucifixion. Did real blood flow from the body that was pinned and nailed to the beams? The nuns repeated many stories about the miracles of Christ and the saints. They told how Christ or God or the Virgin Mother would appear and reveal secrets to good people. Later, great monuments in honor of these good people were constructed and they became saints. I guess I wanted to be a saint and always looked for a sign, a message, of a visitation from either a saint, Mary, or Christ himself, but I guess I didn't make it.

We were told to fast before attending Mass and taking Holy Communion, which sometimes left us dizzy from hunger. Supper was always at five the night before and I did not always get a snack before going to bed. Sometimes I would get dizzy while sitting in the pew waiting for Communion. When a child is dizzy his mind wanders and often his eyes play tricks. I was dizzy. My eyes played tricks. I saw Christ move on the cross. Without a doubt, I was positive He moved. I called a nun and most reverently explained my spiritual experience. I was obviously bound for sainthood as Christ had given me a sign. He moved on the cross. Needless to say, I was ridiculed and shamed. The next morning I was spanked and once again had my mouth washed out, all the while being told in no uncertain terms that I was *not* a saint and *never* would be one. Christ would appear *only* to the innocent and I was surely *not* of that order. My soul was dirty from both lying and having a rich imagination. That harangue ended the nuns, Holy Family School, and Catholicism for me. I begged my father to allow me to attend public school, where I could take various shop courses, such as wood, metal, and print. He agreed, knowing full well I was never going to be a saint or a priest. The nuns had convinced him of that.

three

Peonies, Plums, and Passions

Butternuts and peonies; elms and bleeding hearts; maples and lilies of the valley; a trellis of roses canopies the veranda of a low, charcoal-colored house, home to three aging but nimble spinsters: Florence Graves, Etta Zeller, and Lena Butterfield. Three ladies who held a magic that attracted the neighborhood's children, including the three who lived next door to them in a squatty grass-colored house near the railroad tracks, behind a fattening lilac bush, which scented the area as its blossoms announced summer was here.

No secret that the side garden that sloped to the edge of the drive was an exotic locale. Across warm days of spring and summer, the yard was festooned with ever-changing colors under rich shadows of butternuts, elms, and maples, tapped in the dying days of winter for the sweet juices that would eventually end up on the dining room table of this musty old house crammed with antiques and cats. A daily visit was necessary to the yard to check the flowering and changing of colors and species. Ms. Graves, better known as Aunt Flo, had given me, the boy from the tribe next door, the chore of watering one very special butternut tree. Adults laughed, perhaps with reason, to see a child of five or so with bucket in hand, striking out for the yard to water a tree of some twenty-five feet in height, a fully grown, adult tree. It was my duty, but the obligation was one of pleasure. The tree was my very own, and caring for it was my only true responsibility at that time of my life. I was thrilled that Aunt Flo had such faith in my young abilities. Consequently, I took an enormous interest not only in the butternut but also in the bleeding hearts, the iris, and the other flowers and shrubs that had been carefully nurtured by the elderly spinsters . . . my friends. And decidedly, they *were* my friends, and good friends of my sisters and our parents too. The house was corralled by gardens and shaded by various fruit trees, such as the wild plum at the far end of the vegetable garden and the crabapple between the summer kitchen, as well as by the more formal flower garden, which every season was rowed with gladiolus, dahlias, zinnias, veronica, and bee balm. Often Etta, caretaker of the back garden, would fill my arms with flowers to take across the drive to my mother, who was expecting company, whether it was my grandma, or my aunts from Canada, or my aunts from New Jersey. After helping to pull weeds from around carrots, radishes, squash, and other vegetables, Etta would allow me to pick raspberries and take some home to make my own special dish . . . a sweet reward for backbreaking labors in rows of onions and melons. Etta was generous. She was also an educator.

However, the true educator was Aunt Flo, who showered marvels in an antique parlor in which she sat two girls, Agnes and Mary, down at the piano and taught them how to finger the keys and how to work the pedals. Me? Well, I was a different kind of student. My fingers never relaxed to the keys . . . frozen shut, they made noise, not music. I was not to be abandoned, though. She observed how I enjoyed the Sunday comics, comic books, Tarzan books, whatever simple kind of reading materials came near those nonmusical fingers. Between the formal parlor and a bizarre dining room, in a kind of cubbyhole alcove, were stacks of newspapers maintained on stout tables. Yellowed, dusty, covered in cat hair, both ageless and ageing, they dated back to at least the turn of the century, collectors' items in these mid-1930s. I looked at this ragged pile furtively. A journalist in the budding. A writer, she supposed, dreamed. When younger, Aunt Flo had been a schoolmarm in a one-room, red-painted schoolhouse like the one about which my mother told me. She not only walked, trudged through winter blizzards, to get to this schoolhouse, she chopped wood for its potbellied stove and drew water from the creek so that her children would have something to drink. She always brought extra food in her lunch pail . . . just in case a student or two had arrived hungry and empty-handed. Even though it was a dairy-farming community, there was poverty and hunger. Many of her charges lived on tenant farms, their fathers lazy, drinkers, or otherwise unable to eke out a living from the earth.

Aunt Flo thoroughly enjoyed telling me her mental anthology of stories about the schoolhouse and about the boys and girls who had attended it over the years. She had been an excellent teacher endowed with great compassion and outright love for the young, the opposite of the dour nuns I encountered at school. Each year she lived with a different farm family as part of her teaching salary . . . or, as we would say today, a perk. Now, I think of her stories in relation to some of the writing of both Willa Cather and Mari Sandoz. She was a storyteller and a good one. And she loved to read . . . those huge stacks of newspapers in the alcove—with others upstairs, stacked away in a forbidden bedroom—and books. The parlor was lined with glass-doored bookcases containing hundreds of books, many of them bound in leather. Odd, but I don't recall titles on the shelves other than the classics. Often Aunt Flo would take a dusty, yet sweet-smelling leather-bound volume out of a case and place it in my hands. That was a thrill and proved that she trusted not only my hands, but also my mind, which would one day contain the contents of that book. She taught me to love and care for the physical books and, correspondingly, for the marvelous and magical words they contained. My fingers might be frozen on the piano's keyboard, but they were not averse to turning the pages of a book.

That parlor was a museum. No settee or couch. Straight chairs with soft cushions; the piano, of course; a handsome marble-top table in the center of the shadowed room . . . rarely did light filter into the space due to the rose trellis and low porch roof. I remember porcelain vases from Asia, Chinese silk hangings, brilliant in color despite the accumulated dust of many years. There were figurines, Japanese dolls, which we children were neither allowed to play with nor to touch. Where they came from, how they were collected, I never learned that secret. There was an old-fashioned card table set up near the front window . . . the only light came from it, and at this particular table we played cards; ironically, we even played "Old Maid" with Lena Butterfield, the oldest of the three spinsters, who came from a very prominent Watertown family. Her family home stood for many years on Washington Street, a gorgeous mansion, yellow and hugely impressive. Lena was, as they said back then, retarded; she was a blood niece of Aunt Flo and was fostered out into her care. There were times when Lena actually was spanked for committing some minor infraction of household law. She was then in her early seventies. But as young as we were, my sisters and I regarded her as an equal . . . except when playing "Old Maid." Some confession is overdue: we always cheated the poor darling. She always lost. She was always crowned the old maid. She loved it and would giggle for hours after that she was the old maid. Lena was the first of the three to die.

The parlor was magical, the foyer was dark and troublesome; the second floor was forbidden unless you needed the bathroom, and then you'd be taken by hand and led quickly up and down to take care of your business. Whichever of the three ladies had escorted you would also stay in the room, albeit with her head turned, as nature took its course. The dining room, kitchen, and pantry were chaos and havoc. A ten-foot table stood dead center, surrounded by chairs. The table was piled with all the condiments normally found in a refrigerator: mustard, catsup, mayonnaise, jams and jellies, pickles, apple butter, peanut butter. There was also a mound of dinnerware and silverware in the center, directly under a large hanging Tiffany lamp. Aunt Flo usually made us sandwiches of either catsup or mustard and we declared them absolutely delicious. In our father's house we would have never deigned to eat such food: "No meat, no eat." It was joyful sitting at this huge buffet-like table with a catsup sandwich and a china cup of chamomile tea . . . well, really just a drop of tea in a cup otherwise filled with warm milk. It was sweetly delicious. We children preferred it to any other beverage. Upon reaching adulthood we learned that those jams and mustards were often moldy, and the bread was always green around the crust. My father asked how we could bear to eat such things. It didn't bother us at the time . . . the occasions always had a party atmosphere to us. We were guests at that incredible table. Today, thinking back, I can't help but remember the audacious dining-room table set for a wedding in Dickens's *Great Expectations*. The wedding never took place, and the wedding cake just remained in place for years, hung with cobwebs, rotting in disappointment, and (in the movie version, at least) a rat scampering in and out of it.

The kitchen also contained a huge table, a round one that (like so many other places in that house) collected newspapers. It was also ordained to be the eating spot for those cats that were allowed downstairs. There seemed to be hundreds of cats in that house at the time, but obviously it could not have been more than a dozen or so. The cats that were pregnant or in heat were kept in secrecy of the upstairs rooms, where there were not heaps of ragged newspapers and where there were little tins and plates of cat food . . . mainly chopped boiled potatoes and perhaps a string or two of whatever meat or fish had been prepared for dinner the night before. The pantry was a dark cave and contained a sink and cabinets where the dishes piled on the dining-room table might have once been stored. I don't remember an icebox or refrigerator, which perhaps explains the mold. After Aunt Flo and Lena passed, Etta had the house exhumed. Nearly everything was tossed out, including all of the cats but one. It reeked of felines and stale food. Everything was cleaned, washed, polished, and sprayed with Lysol. I went back there as a college student, but couldn't quite accept the new beauty of the rooms, especially the parlor.

Etta Zeller was a very special woman. She was born somewhere in the Midwest . . . perhaps Ohio . . . and was related to Aunt Flo on the opposite side of Lena. She worked as the office manager for a paper company in Dexter, New York, until her retirement. She greatly enjoyed the company of young people, though not small children, who always seemed to be underfoot. Even to them, though, she was never rude or unkind. She wished to live in a more intelligent world and pursued politics and the arts. Eventually she opened the second floor and turned it into an apartment, which she rented to young married couples until her death in the late 1950s. She was an elegant woman. You might picture her as a character in a novel by Edith Wharton or Henry James. Aristocratic, though landless and moneyless, but blessed with "good blood" nevertheless.

Butternuts and peonies. They spell surprise, childhood enchantment, and if the realm they levitated us into was not exactly fairyland—pulling weeds in their garden was very real and backbreaking work—there still was a rich, sensuous quality of life that beckoned and stimulated our childish imaginations, needful of music and the thrills to be found in books, stories. They were loyal women, unforgettable, kind in offering of flowers and raspberries, understanding with the gift of the butternut, lovable and patient in music lessons. Their house was a sanctuary for young tots already confused by life and coping as best they could with the pains that all children know and suffer. Aunt Flo was a catalyst; Etta, a source of strength through her moral fiber and work ethic; Lena, oh Lena . . . do I dare say, the humor, the comic relief? She made my sisters and me think of ourselves as adults. They are inscribed on my brain, burned into my imagination, and chiseled into my personal sense of value. I don't think either ever went to church. I'm not sure that they belonged to a church, but they were the only true Christians I have ever known in my lifetime. From the bottom of my very being I thank them for having been our neighbors. If I plant a geranium today or pluck a wild raspberry, if I look up into a maple or a dying elm, I know the focus to see the beauty in them was given to me by these three ladies in retirement. Soon after Etta's death, the city bought the crumbling gray house with the rose trellis, the butternut, and the plum trees. It was torn down with sledgehammers, bulldozed into memory alone. And the grass-colored house next door with the fat lilac bush that already belonged to the city? Well, it too was torn down, leaving only colored dreams behind.

The three ladies were non-Indian, most likely as WASP-y as you could be, but their morals and ethics were grooved, defined, and executed. They remain vivid pictures in my mind with the clarity of a fine, aged wine. The sight of an iris along the shore of my hometown lake will bring forth those delights of childhood in the charcoaled house, although I have developed an aversion to eating catsup sandwiches.

four

Friends and Idols

I took my friends from among the Audet, Newman, and Young families who lived on the opposite side of the railroad tracks that frequently were our playground. When the trains were zooming down the rails, we placed our precious pennies on them to see what the great weight of the passing engine would do to the coins. It was the Depression and pennies came only rarely into our hands. We also played in Etta Zeller's large stand of plum trees, a stand of sapling poplars in our own backyard, and a vacant lot across the tracks near my friends' houses. Theirs were nothing more than row houses, owned by the same kind landlord who in those difficult days would knock on the separate doors at Christmastime and deliver a basket of fruit and maybe some canned goods. I can't but believe he often did without getting the rent in return. We played mostly in the vacant lots . . . benign games like marbles, less benign ones like mumblety-peg, and my schoolyard curse, baseball. I was not too proficient at it and deserved the taunts and rancor of my fellow teammates. We camped overnight with old pillows and ratty blankets too shameful to use on a guest bed, and we played cowboys and Indians. Naturally, I was always the Indian, even though Carl Young and his sister were Indian as well. I was always chosen to be the Indian who was roped to a stake and set afire, sometimes with a real fire with flames darting around my feet. Of course, my playmates always said they would not set the dry grasses around my feet to flame. But they lied. Many a day Mrs. Newman had to drop her work and come rushing out to the lot to save my life. She, indeed, scolded all of us . . . the others laughing, guffawing . . . and I was in tears . . . "They made me do it."

Another confession: Carl had a much younger sister, I don't remember her name, and she was most ticklish. When she was tickled, she wet her pants. Well, *that* proved to be real fun. In the poplar saplings behind my father's house also stood a huge railroad tie. We'd go there and drag the poor child with us and start tickling her. She'd pee and wet her pants; then, crying with embarrassment, she would pull off her panties. That was the real fun for us, because then we could see how she differed from us boys.

Etta Zeller's plum trees were a grand place for scurrilous activity. Within the trees we were hidden by leaves and trunks and ripening fruit. Unless someone, a parent or Etta, were standing at the very edge of the copse, we could not be observed. Even Aunt Flo could not have spotted us from her kitchen window, nor could my mother from our back porch. It was there that we boys proved our manhood. It was there that, ever so often, down came our trousers and out came the penis ruler. We had to measure how large we were growing. I remember holding Jack's and placing the cold ruler against the foreskin. Two inches. Hadn't grown that week. However, a weird sensation arose from my fingers and up into my loins . . . I flushed, but didn't realize why. He seemed to have no problem with measuring mine or Carl's or that of any other young lad that hid in the plums with us. We were never caught. Our curiosity and our manhood were safe. Years later, I learned from other male friends that they had accomplished similar acts of bravery out of dire necessity to see if they were truly normal human beings with all the proper male accoutrements.

As I said, Carl was Indian. It seems now that my father told me that his family came from Onondaga. Another family also had moved into the neighborhood and they hailed from Kahnawake, so I may have Carl's home reserve mixed in my memory. Carl was dark, whereas I was and remain light. His thick black hair was enviable, as was the tone of his skin. He was a handsome young boy and he was my friend. During our clandestine gatherings in the plum bushes, I never had the courage to measure his privates. We were close friends and that simply wouldn't do. There were days when I would not share my playtime with anyone but Carl. We'd even sleep nights wrapped in those ratty blankets on my front porch. In his row house there wasn't room on the porch to sleep; there was barely sufficient space for a chair. But my porch was shaded into privacy by the great lilac bush. Very little sleeping was accomplished there, however. We talked, told stories, dreamed across the night, which always ended in dampness, the fall of the dew.

Sadly, our friendship ended in war. Two factions of the neighborhood's boys decided to have a fight. Carl was on one side and I the other. Having identified our respective enemies, we gathered stones and small rocks, marched to the railroad tracks in phalanx, aimed and fired. Carl was the first to be struck . . . by my stone. I was the second to be hit . . . by Carl's stone . . . in the face. I bled. I cried, and I ran home into the house where my mother was baking bread. She washed the wound, told me to stay indoors and find a book to read. She promptly told my father about our war the moment he entered the kitchen that evening after work. He didn't spank me but gave me a serious talk. "You don't hurt your friends. Friends do not war against each other. You must never pick up stones again because they fly home and strike back. What goes out comes around." He was right. The tragedy was not so much our physical wounds, painful though they were. I never spoke to or saw Carl again. The next week his family moved away; his father needed to find work. I have looked for my friend all these many years to say how sorry I am to have thrown the rock and struck him. In fact, I have not seen any of those boys for these many years and do not know if they still exist in this crazy world.

The Audets were French-Canadian Indians from somewhere in Quebec. Cree, maybe. I don't know. Mohawk, maybe . . . from Oka or Kahnawake. I don't know. I know only that they were a very large family, like the Youngs, and were very poor. Both parents spoke little English, and Mr. Audet worked as often as there was work to be obtained through the Work Progress Administration. My father emphasized the fact that they were poor, not to shame them but to remind me how to act. He said when at their house I should never accept food because they didn't have enough to share. If food was present, I should simply say I was not hungry, that my mother had just fed me, excuse myself from their company and go home. I held off from these invitations, but it wasn't always easy. Mrs. Audet was a good woman and couldn't bear to see any child hungry. One day she insisted I sit down at the lunch table. She served macaroni with lard. I had a hard time eating it, not because of the taste but because I knew I was taking food that I shouldn't. Figuratively, I held my nose and gulped down, swallowing, a spoonful or two, sheepishly exclaimed I had to go to the bathroom, and ran across the tracks up the gully and into my mother's kitchen. She wasn't there. My sister Mary said she was downtown at J. J. Newberry's and Woolworth's trying on hats again. My two older sisters were both tattlers, and Agnes told my father that I had eaten food at the Audet table despite his prohibition. I was whipped, and she was scolded strongly for having tattled. Actually the Audet children were not my friends . . . they were all much older, but as my sisters were friendly with their two younger daughters, I still somehow figured within the kindly Audet household.

I did have heroes in my midst as a small kid. Two heroes, in fact: Cigar and . . . well, let's call the other boy Rocco. They were both special, very special to my childish thinking. Rocco was a year or two older, but because he continued to get failing grades year after year, he ended up in the same classroom with me. His grandmother ran an Italian grocery store, and although his family was not poor, he dressed in rather ragged, if not seedy, clothes. He often had holes in his pants and wore dirty shirts. He might have been a hippie long before that conspicuously shabby style of dress became fashionable. I think the nuns despised him. I *know* he hated them. They were constantly spanking him for being truant, for being sassy, for standing too long in the boys' rooms, and for writing words on the hallway walls. He never completed any homework and usually refused to answer when called upon by the teacher. He was an out-and-out bad boy in a way that would earn him the label of "at-risk youth" if he were growing up today. He had been sent to the boys' reformatory once or twice, though I have no idea what crime he committed . . . unless it was truancy. He had a kind of nasty way of speaking from the left side of his mouth, and he almost always smelled of garlic.

I worshipped the ground he dismissively spat on, and though I walked in his physical tracks in emulation, I did not dare talk back to the nuns, or come to school in tattered clothes, or pee on the bathroom wall, or play hooky. It would never do. My father would punish me after the nuns were finished with my backside (or front, as they had made clear). I certainly admired Rocco. When I thought no one was looking, I aped his style; I even said I loved garlic, though I had no idea what it was. There was a sensual quality to his walk, his sway, his undulation. I even attempted to copy that. I must confess, once I dared to sneak behind a huge sign to rip my trousers, a pair of over-the-knee corduroys that I disliked intensely and was forced to wear. When I showed up to school with my torn pants visible above my brown woolen stockings, I was the laughingstock of the classroom. Even Rocco laughed and that crushed me. Years later I heard he had reformed and was most successful as the manager and proprietor of his grandmother's grocery store.

My second living hero was Cigar, a kid probably twelve years old, four years older than myself at the time. I had no idea where Cigar lived. On Saturday mornings he always appeared at the ice skating rink at what was then called the old "Silk Mill," which formerly had been a box factory. He appeared, but always without skates. He'd stand at the edge of the ice, fists shoved into his pants pockets, and stare at us with unmistakable hostility. He wouldn't stay the entire morning, probably because he was cold, wearing only a very light fall jacket. He probably hadn't had any breakfast either, perhaps not even coffee. Cigar wasn't very tall, and people said he had a mean and hungry look. My thought was that he was super. He didn't seem to give a damn about anything or anybody; he was his own man, even without ice skates. Spotting his leave-taking, I'd sneak behind him and follow with wonder, curious where he was going, where he lived. Several times I caught him stopping by the entrance to the rink to unbutton his pants and spray his saffron water onto the snow like the white bear in Denise Levertov's marvelous poem "To the Reader." Perhaps this memory is the reason that poem remains a favorite of mine, and why I have used it in creative writing classes for decades.

So why was Cigar called "Cigar"? Well, even though he now reminds me of a white bear in a poem, what I have failed to mention is that Cigar was a young black man, something that already made him stand out in northern New York. I was not the only one who observed him nonchalantly peeing into the snow, and whenever we did so we inevitably took particular notice of his privates. His penis was long and dark and shaped like a cigar . . . hence, his nickname, a testament both to our rather limited horizons and our overly literal imaginations. But his nickname was not a jibe or a joke; I was proud and more than a little envious that he could just whip it out and pee onto the crusted snow and feel no shame, no guilt. By then I was consumed by shame and burning with guilt at so many things. Without intending to, he taught me something about standing up against the world and about simple, yet sweet revenge.

Having not yet had much experience of the wider world, Rocco and Cigar were celebrities as far as I was concerned.

five

Sensations, Dreams, Visions

My childhood up until junior high school had a sensuous quality enhanced by a variety of stimuli: my mother's bread baking in the oven; my Aunt Jennie's blackberry pie steaming on the dinner table; Etta Zeller's kaleidoscopic fairyland of a flower garden; the Catholic nuns' rulers sharply striking against my tenderest flesh; the smelly fish and bloody game that my father brought home from summer waters and autumn woods; the allergies to eggs, dust, goldenrod that compromised my eating and breathing; the smell of horse flesh after a long canter, an abiding part of my love of horseback riding despite my early mishaps. One of the most important sensations, though, is one that I continue to remember and that has inspired my thoughts and words for decades: the scent of wild June strawberries.

Years after she moved away from it, my mother's old family homestead had been sold to two young men who were avid hunters. They wanted the woods on the land for deer and pheasant hunting, so they demolished the house and built a camp in its place. That demolition broke my heart. The house, always in need of paint, was a marvelous bastion of sensory impressions: tastes and touches, smells and hearing, and viewings. The old house contained many bedrooms and my favorite was my grandmother's boudoir . . . it was a true boudoir. Rarely were we children allowed to spend a night in her great bed with the tick mattress. But it was a joyful event when Grandma said "yes." The room was at the front of the house, over the formal parlor that jutted out from the frame. It seemed to extend over the garden and became for me a part of the front lawn. Large, airy, the brightest room in the house, the windows faced the yard, with the apple orchard to the left and the drive bordered by a continuous circular yellow rosebush to the right. The adjacent fields of June-ripening wild strawberries bore a contagious aroma. This was before I learned the importance of the wild strawberry to Iroquois people. The first natural fruit of the eastern spring thousands of years ago came to be the symbol of rejuvenation and a property of healing. Their scent made my senses more acutely aware of apple blossoms, the roses Grandpa had planted years and years before, the mown grasses, the smell of freshly washed linen drying in sunny air. Given the rare opportunity of sleeping or napping in Grandma's room, I became so affected by these scents, especially the strawberries. While lying between the fresh sheets, I was often wakeful for most of the night because of my overactive olfactory glands.

Color, too, became an exquisite commodity. I recall dark green watermelons fattening in Aunt Jennie's garden near the peanut plants that never yielded her a harvest. She enjoyed experimenting with various exotic plants. Once she attempted a coffee tree, but it turned out to be a crushing failure. Not a leaf sprang from the earth. Iris and blue chicory became favorite flowers, as did black elderberries dangling in the spokes of the afternoon sun; Uncle Bert's white mare pulling a sled-load of wood through a thick emerald forest; the pink birthday cake I couldn't eat because of the egg allergy. I have disliked the color pink all my life.

The senses became utterly important to me as a child, though they did so without my truly knowing, understanding why I was moved by particular sensations: flight of the bat under the porch roof of summer; electrical storms; the feel of beach sand running through my fingers; the joy of a tick mattress; rich whipped cream on my tongue from Uncle Frank's cows; the craggy trunk of a hickory tree; a field of brilliant hawkweed; the acrid, nutty smell of sweat on the hired men as they pitched hay or thrashed wheat; the shine of scales of a rainbow trout; all the beauty of a black willow; the rise of green hills; thin white rapids of Cold Creek; sails on the lake; my father's hunting boots and the shine of his rifles, oiled and ready for the kill; muted browns of rabbit fur, or the sheen of beagles' coats. When I was very young, I found comfort in every aspect of a stream that flowed past my house: the sonorous clattering of the waters; the trout swimming within; the sand and smoothly dark rocks over which the clear creek leisurely flowed; the black willows shading the ripples, standing guard along the shore. I was even drawn to the muskrats that lived in the hollows of the embankment, the muskrats who swiftly dashed across the brimming creek like arrows moving through heavy winds.

When I was in high school I painted with oils. Not well, not interestingly, but in a poor imitation of Grandma Moses, who was extremely popular at the time. My father and his friends seemed pleased, almost enamored, by my art and encouraged me to go off to an art school. I knew better. Colorist I was, draftsman I was not. My horses looked like dogs and my dogs resembled stones in a field. There was a time during which I was quite taken with design and I designed many floor plans. It was fun, but not to be taken seriously, and yet my father managed to sell for a small sum one of my plans to a friend. I think, perhaps, I was being patronized. No music, no art. I was stuck with being the budding journalist that Aunt Flo had supposed I might be.

When I arrived at Shakespeare's plays and John Keats's odes and songs, I was bowled over. My love of color and affinity for the senses had prepared me for these two great poets, whose works I was encouraged to read by Aunt Flo. They remain friends, as heroes residing curiously in the same corner of my brain alongside Rocco, Cigar, and the three elderly spinsters. Rocco gave me the strength to endure and survive the wrath and punishment of not only the nuns of St. Joseph, but of the world in general; Cigar gave me a strong and lasting sense of pride, even though my shyness may hide this character trait. Aunt Flo, dear good Aunt Flo, brought beauty to my years.

Like all young children, I was regularly bedded with illnesses . . . even though some of them were manufactured. I was downed by measles, scarlet fever, and the chicken pox, which subsequently lay dormant for some fifty years, when it reared up into the ugly rash and piercing pain of shingles while I was teaching in British Columbia at the En'owkin Centre. Colds often took their due, while vertigo was a problem for me in the sixth grade and caused fainting spells. I once fell down the staircase at Holy Family. Bloody noses occurred frequently, and, of course, I dealt with my ever-present allergies. Like most children of the time, I suffered from toothaches and the subsequent extractions and fillings. But never has a wisdom tooth caused me trouble, even though my sisters suffered greatly with their wisdom teeth. As an adult, I wrote a poem about a particular fever I had:

VISITATION

Fever and Chill
chill and fever.

I knew what oranges were
though I had never sunk a tooth into one.

Grandma Parker walked
into the room with an orange
        peeled
for sucking juices.

I lay back into my five years
and dreamed in death.

The morning sun healed
what fever and chill remained.

But my father growled:
"The kid's still sick.
Doesn't he know
she's been dead two years."

Odd, spectral Grandma Parker had been dead two years, and oranges were most rare in northern New York in winter. In dreams all manner of acts can take place. If you believe . . . and the young have great faith, or certainly this young lad did . . . cures may be received from the ghostly presence of the dead, especially one loved as deeply as a great-grandmother. Dreams are deeply significant to Native American people, particularly Iroquois, and especially to me. I think I have found the key . . . with some help . . . to deciphering my dreams: the subconscious attempting to slowly inform the conscious mind of some matter of import . . . at times a prism of technicolored, miasmic, visionary illusions . . . the island in the stream, the creek flashing down the mountain shoulder, or in fantasy itself. I was always a dreamer, and at times remain a "daydreamer," though such woolgathering is not at all the same thing. Dreams are not to be toyed with, misinterpreted, ridiculed, mocked, or dismissed. They could predict danger, possible disaster.

Grandma Parker was conjured in my fever and chill, in dream or vision. How deeply the illness took hold of me that night I cannot know or remember, but it was serious. I believe it was a bout with scarlet fever, which I continuously contracted by playing in the winter slush of the gully between the grass-green house and the railroad tracks. It was a fun place to slide and skate when the trickles of water had frozen. My mother could not keep me out of the gully. Grandmothers often exude love and strength, cures and comfort. Children are aware of these portentous qualities, and I summoned her to my dream to cure my illness . . . which she did. Vision . . . the climb up hill or mountain to fast and dream, the study of spirit in wind or water, touching earth . . . has been written about far more successfully by others, like Peter Blue Cloud or the classic rendering of the Lakota holy man Black Elk. I can add little.

In my later youth and adult life, I was pretty much free of disease and illness. I did suffer a heart attack at the age of forty-four while living in Brooklyn, New York. This was very strange. I was working as a waiter in a neighborhood pub, and discovered I was occasionally losing the feeling in my left hand. I had some pain, and I felt nauseous much of the time. So I consulted a local neighborhood doctor who insisted that it must be a brain tumor that needed, demanded, an immediate operation. I scoffed. A night or two later, a friend conducted me to Cumberland Hospital in Brooklyn because of these recurring symptoms. There, an East Indian doctor, young and cautious, responded that there were heart problems; his assistant, a white, Anglo doctor, said I was merely lazy and trying to avoid work. He insisted there was nothing wrong with me other than an ulcer pressing against the heart: "Take some antacids and return to work." The next night, at 3:00 a.m., rising out of a bed in sweat, nauseous and in dire pain, I called a friend and said I was going down to the street to find a taxi to take me to Long Island College Hospital, a few blocks from my apartment. I remember being wheeled in, being undressed, and then at some later point being awakened (I have no idea when) by a cardiologist, Dr. ——, who was looking over me. No soft smile, no gentle hand-holding, no comfort through the eyes. Later, Dr. —— inquired what I recalled of my experience while I had blacked out. It was weird. Like Tantalus in Tartarus, I found myself in a shining yellow world, austere in sound, without smell. The yellow light bore down heavily into my vision. Something, without touching, continued to pull me upward to a high, pointed hill. I would fall back down. Again and again I would be tugged up the hill only to slip backward. It seemed an eternity. Many weeks later, after I was released from the hospital, Dr. —— again asked me of the experience, and I again related my mythically tinged tale of the yellow world. This time he smiled and responded: "I was pleading with you to live. You didn't want to stay in our world. I would not release you. I was determined not to lose you. You were totally exhausted, which helped to cause your illness. It was, and remains, my mission to save a poet. I continued to plead until your eyelashes fluttered and you awakened." It had been a virus, he believed, causing a problem with my heart that normally affects men much older than the middle-aged man I was then. It was the disease of an old man.

He saved my life. I did as he suggested. I wrote out my heart and my pain, instead. Since then I have been comparatively healthy, though I've also been pulled back after approaching that yellow world again on a couple of occasions.

six

Looking for Home

It rained the night I ran away. An angry rain.

The rain struck rooftops, sidewalks, autumn earth with such force I knew that I was not the only thing in existence that was troubled. Rain pelted against windowpanes, splattered down eaves, ran in whirls and circles through gutters, blustered down drains.

The world was drenched. My spirit was drenched.

My world and the world were coming apart, and this soggy world was neither of my own making nor of my desire.

As a child I was shy. My two older sisters certainly helped develop this particular characteristic from which I have suffered most of my adult life, despite appearing loud and arrogant at times. The brawl, the bluster, the stomp has always been self-defense, my best imitation of how I thought Rocco or Cigar would respond to the world's provocations. My mother was a rather quiet woman, my father usually soft-spoken except when angry; his firmness, especially as he grew older, could be frightening, and I often cowered before him. He was older, wiser, more assured, somewhat defiant, not merely of certain conventions, but of humans generally. He was successful in his chosen work, not only successful, but happy and proud. I was not proud, not happy, and had no reason to feel successful as a child. I had been deeply intimidated by my mother regarding the flaws of men, of overt masculinity, so I acquired an offensive defense: shyness. While I was still quite young, on nights after my sisters had trudged off to bed involuntarily, my mother would take me into her bedroom and sit at the bottom of her bed. From there, we would stare out into the night. In winter we watched snow fall, tiny flakes as insignificant as myself. She would point off in the distance and beckon my sight to an automobile parked a block or two away. She said that my father sat in that car and that he wasn't alone. She said he was with another woman, a girlfriend. Mama would tell me how bad men were, thoughtless, inconsiderate, driven by sexual urges to commit the most heinous of sins and crimes. And she told me that my father was playing foul.

I did not know if this was true, or whether it was even him in that car kissing a woman other than my mother. I had only her word, her say-so, and her fears, which over time became mine. This indoctrination became the foundation for my shyness, particularly my shyness around women and most particularly women of strength and authority, like teachers. It also colored my imagination and intellect. I have wondered if we men are actually all "bad," all capable of demolishing a woman's femininity, or worse, her entire sense of self. Perhaps my mother was correct in her assumptions. Many feminists to this moment feel the same ideas rankle within their minds. Perhaps they are right. I can't really say. The only thing I know is that I would have been a different man if my mother had not sat me on the edge of her bed on those snowy winter nights and programmed me into thinking men were inherently bad. What my father was doing was without a doubt wrong. If he no longer cared about, let alone loved, my mother, he should have been honest and forthright with her, and separated or worked things out through some form of counseling. He did not. He was a womanizer. It didn't mean he did not love my mother. I have always believed he did . . . but has it been simply necessary for me to continue telling myself this, to hold on to this belief for some handle on sanity?

My mother, putting this collective guilt on me as a child, augmented the guilt the nuns at Holy Family indelibly burnt into my mind. Every morning after prayer, and before the structured class commenced, the nuns would tell us how Father Isaac Jogues was brutally slaughtered in the mid-1600s. They told us he was beheaded by the Mohawk men, having first been tortured by the Mohawk women. Such a "kind good man," and how "dreadfully savage" the Mohawks had been to this "saint," and "didn't I feel ashamed of this history?" I certainly *didn't* feel ashamed or guilty at the beginning of first grade, I know that much. But I became guilty as time wore on. Yes, it certainly was my fault that this good saint, Father Isaac Jogues, missionary to the Mohawks, had died so cruel and heathenish a death. Naturally, the nuns failed to relate *why* he had been put to death by the Nation's chiefs. First of all, he was French, and therefore not to be trusted; the French had not only slaughtered Mohawks in ambush in 1609, but upon entering the Native villages later on, they brought all sorts of diseases that killed off large populations of Mohawks and other Iroquois people, everything from colds to smallpox. On arriving in the village they systematically started to missionize, to convert the Native people to Catholicism from their own perfectly good and workable religions. They attacked the minds of the women first, then the small children. They also relayed information to the French crown about the numbers of Native warriors, the quality of beaver and mink fur, trade routes by land and water . . . and they did so knowing that the English crown also had eyes upon the region for the same reasons of conquest and domination. Yes, the nuns failed to speak of these horrors that the Jesuits committed upon Native peoples, and I learned to feel guilty instead for the fate of saintly Isaac Jogues.

The guilt stuck with me. Night after night, throughout my life these horror stories and the guilt persisted in my nightmares. At the same time, my mother's influence was doing more of the same. One mustn't forget the Jesuits were males. The Mohawk warriors were male as well. And my father was a male. It took a series of persona poems that I wrote years later about the story of Isaac Jogues to obliterate the guilt the nuns and my mother had so steadfastly burnt into my mind. Poetry is absolutely not therapy . . . no matter what reading Robert Lowell or Sylvia Plath might make some believe . . . but it can purge out thoughts and feelings that have no other way to be released from the deepest reaches of the mind.

In my earliest childhood years, it was a house of women in which I was raised . . . with another house of three women next door. My father was seldom home. He worked much of the time at his job with the city of Watertown, staying late and earning many overtime hours. Weekends he hunted or fished, and weekend nights he was "out on the town." In the early days of my life, my mother was often with him on those weekend night excursions, but some unseen, unspoken confrontation must have taken place between them and he started to leave her home. He went out on his own, dressed in a white shirt and tie in a tailored suit. She said he often came home near dawn with lipstick on his collar . . . another telltale sign of being bad.

My oldest sister, Agnes, had left my father's house because of their heated arguments over one of her boyfriends. My father demanded that she no longer see him, as he was sure that the young man in question was not good enough for his daughter. My father was sure that the young man, a French Indian, was loose, lazy, and would end up a bum. She disobeyed my father's command, and finally he told her to leave. A few years later she married him, and he proved my father's prediction about him completely wrong. John became a successful airplane mechanic and a devoted husband and father right up to the day of his unfortunate early death. My other sister, Mary, was also seeing a young man of whom my father disapproved. My mother did not share his misgivings, however. What were his daughters and wife doing? Why did they go against his wishes, his better sense, his common sense, and his knowledge of these two young men? There were brutal arguments between Mary and my father, but he would lose a second time. She also ended up marrying him, and Pat, as he was nicknamed, appeared to be a good provider and good husband from what we could tell.

Having had his will sidestepped twice, my father was determined that I would listen to his counsel. I would not end up in a bad marriage. To make this happen, he did not chain me to my bedroom wall, nor beat me into submission. He attempted a different method, giving in to most of my demands, adolescent foolishness, and needs, and tolerating what he considered my peculiar character. I was sensitive and imaginative, and, unfortunately, both creative and shy. The possibly pragmatic enthusiasm he expressed for my juvenile daubs and sketches would be tested further as I found my way to poetry.

My parents separated when I was nine years old. Some years later they divorced. My father went to work in Rome, New York; my mother stayed in Watertown, working at various jobs, renting apartments for her and me for the two years following the separation. I enjoyed those years with her even though we rarely spent time together. She worked nights and I schooled days . . . meaning that I needed to get my own supper and, after homework, to tuck myself into bed. When I opened a can of tomato soup or fried some hamburgers, I thought I was really getting supper ready for the two of us, but she rarely came home to eat. Bologna was good to a young boy's taste buds, but eating alone wasn't fun. So after the sandwich or soup or whatever can I'd open was ready to eat, I'd toss it out and contented myself with what the school cafeteria had served me for lunch. We were then living in a dark apartment on Massey Street in Watertown that was permeated by strong smells, some good, some not. The sink coughed up an odd odor of old drainpipes or, perhaps, garbage. But my mother's bedroom smelled of her perfumes and rouge, her lipsticks and hair ointments. That was pleasant. I spent time in her room listening to her radio. I slept on a wicker couch in the living room, spare and frightening, with bare walls painted. The paint was so old and dusty that several lamps could not brighten the room.

One night she came home early from work. There was a man with her in an army uniform. She introduced us and said she had the night off and that they were going out on the town. Little did I know that years later he would become my stepfather. Martin was stationed at Pine Camp, now known as Fort Drum. He was in the tank corps, and his regiment was waiting orders to ship out to the European war, that is, World War II. When at last his orders came, my mother announced matter-of-factly that she was going to live with her three sisters in Bayonne, New Jersey. She couldn't take me with her, but would later send for me. In the meantime, I would go to Syracuse and stay with her girlfriend, who was from there and had recently had been working in Watertown. I'd have lots of fun in their house, and they would teach me Indian ways, which my father still had not as of then. Then my mother left. The Onondaga woman came for me in her car and helped me pack my few things. My mother had put all her belongings in storage, except for the clothes she needed, and cosmetics, things of that nature. I didn't have much, as most of my books, toys, and clothes had remained in my father's house. It seemed that I lived with the Onondaga family an eternity, yet thinking back on it, it must have only been a matter of days. When we left Watertown, it was crisp October. Warm days. Cool nights. Leaves underfoot to be scuffled while walking or piled up in play.

Once we arrived in Syracuse, I assumed I'd be registered for a school, though it had not come up in any conversation between my new foster parents and me. I moped around all day while they worked. Then it rained. Rain is sad, it depresses me even to this moment. It means loneliness, it means desperation. Truly, if it falls in April, it makes the May flowers, and so forth, but tell that to an aching boy who has first lost his father and then been abandoned by his mother. Orphaned, even if not by death. It won't work. I have never liked rain.

A vivid memory: The woman stood at her kitchen stove, the Onondaga woman; she was cooking fry bread for her husband, for her children, and for me. Grease in the skillet spattered her apron and hissed against the exposed flesh of her arm. She called out a painful ouch. I watched her closely as she smiled down on her small children playing around her shoes. She was nice and had been nice to me . . . the fostered boarder. They meant well . . . her husband, the little children . . . and naturally she meant to care very well for me. She'd given me a comfortable bed on the couch, fed me some good-tasting soup, made cookies, and now, that night, she was making fry bread for us all. We'd dip it in maple syrup. I remember she had made sausage and boiled potatoes smothered in the sausage drippings earlier for supper. It was good. She was good. She was young, not over thirty, pale-complexioned; her dark hair was fluffy around her ears and cheeks. She was pretty, and her flower-patterned dress with white roses and bluets accented her prettiness. The children, five and six, were pale-skinned like their mother, but black-haired with big brown eyes. She talked to me in soft words. She said how Hallowe'en would be coming and she'd make candy for us, popcorn balls rolled in molasses, and we'd dress the children and go out trick-or-treating together. I was eleven, the second oldest male in the house, and didn't think much of Hallowe'en pranks anymore: cutting clotheslines, turning over garbage barrels, soaping windows. It wasn't that I had attained too much sophistication for those childish tricks; I was standing near her at the stove, thinking of how I could run out the kitchen door and run away from that family, that house, the fry bread, the abysmal world then surrounding my thin years and thinner body, which ached from loneliness, hurt from having been cast away.

I stole out of the house, never to return. My mother's best friend, Peg Greenwood, also lived in Syracuse, and I understood that one of Peg's friends, a man named Leo, lived near the house where I had been dropped. I wandered through the night looking for Leo's house, reading names at doors and ringing doorbells until at last I found him in an elegant apartment on James Street, which at that time was in a posh neighborhood. He took me in. He'd been warned by Peg, who herself had been warned (presumably by the Onondaga woman) that I was on the loose and might show up at his door. I gather that people were raking the streets for my rain-drenched figure. When Leo opened the door, I was sopping wet, shivering, and cold. I had no jacket. A very tall man, he bent down and hugged my wet figure, pulled me into the room, stripped the wet clothes off me, guided me into a hot steaming tub, and soaked me until whatever fevers and colds might be lurking were safely warded off. He swathed me in one of his own shirts, huge as a tent, and after feeding me hot soup, sent me off to bed. Peg Greenwood phoned my father and told him about my self-inflicted predicament. He phoned Leo and had him take me to Peg's house, once he was assured that I had not come down with an illness from the drenching rain. I stayed with Peg for several months . . . without attending school. Finally, my father made the decision that if my mother did not want me . . . and she had been notified both of my running away and my relocation to Peg's house . . . then I should return north and stay with my aunts instead.

In my wanderings from one would-be home to another, I surely had assumed the semblance of David Copperfield.

seven

To Broadway and Back

My aunts were very kind, even though their houses were filled with whispers that constantly assaulted my ears like sharp points piercing flesh. My grandmother Herrick, never terribly pleased with her second daughter—my mother—argued vehemently with Aunt Jennie and Uncle Frank as to my proper care and upbringing. She had clear views on how best to raise this new burden on the household, this skittish, puberty-fraught boy. She was never crude, but her sentimentality . . . gushing tears over my loneliness . . . began to wear on me after a time. My grandmother was a sobber and a whiner . . . good woman that she was. As a young bride, she had become accustomed to household help, demanding this and that of my grandfather. She had given birth to seven daughters and one son, who did not live through his first year. She did have work, much work, as a mother and as a farmer's wife, but all women did in those early days of the century. Her lot was not exceptional, save the fact that Grandfather Herrick still had some money left from the family fortune, such as it was. Consequently, it was spent on fine furniture for the formal parlor and to hire some household "help." When Grandpa died, he was in debt, mortgaged to the hilt, including his farm, his stock, his cows, and his horses.

Aunt Ruth, one of my two maiden aunts and my mother's younger sister, had stayed on the farm until her father died and then continued living with her married sister, Jennie. Aunt Ruth was a few years older than my sister Agnes, and she was no dour spinster . . . no, she was free and knew how to have fun. A hard worker, she spent her days in the fields, planting and harvesting . . . mainly hay. She spent her evenings in the garden or in berry patches after milking twenty-five head of cows. She put some measure of mirth into my days and played games and did jigsaw puzzles with me after dark. Uncle Frank, the man of the house, was strong but sympathetic. He was my friend and my bulwark against the ladies of the house, especially my grandmother. His compassion was overflowing, and I was desperate for it. He took my side in most familial disagreements concerning my parental poverty, and often I would hear him reinforcing my mother's situation; he always argued that she had an absolute right to life, a life she chose to live . . . but, unfortunately, she had a son.

The time sped by on the farm those months. One day, Aunt Jennie announced that I needed to pack a bag . . . I was leaving for New Jersey. It would be fun, she said . . . a train ride to New York City. My father had decided that because my mother had demanded custody of me in the courtroom at their separation, it was now not only her parental, maternal, and moral duty, but also her legal obligation to assume responsibility of the small boy she had seemingly shrugged off along with northern New York. I do not know how, but he had coerced my mother to accept this decision, and despite some protests, she accepted my return to her bosom. That proved somewhat unfortunate.

I entered school in the eighth grade in Bayonne. They jumped me ahead one grade of where I had been, even though I had missed many days of that year. My cousin Dorothy was to take me in the first morning . . . she was in the same school, the same class, in fact. Whispers behind cupped hands commenced almost immediately. My mother's abandonment of me. The idea I was a quarter-blood Indian . . . in a school of pretty much all Italians and Irish . . . my father's Irishness apparently played no role in his absence. Dorothy was smart and popular with the kids; I proved to be neither. Teachers came down on me like the horrid rains in Syracuse. I was determined to run away once more, but instead of taking up my proverbial hobo-pack on a stick, I simply skipped school each morning. My mother gave me money for the bus and for lunch, and each morning I did board a bus . . . just not one bound for school. Instead, I walked out to what was then Hudson Boulevard (now John F. Kennedy Boulevard) and went off to New York City.

I was particularly keen on Times Square, because that's where the theater stage shows were, the *legitimate* theater . . . and the movie stars. Klieg lights, limelight, starlight-blinded vision. I soon found friends sympathetic to my thinking, and we were on the hunt together. No, not to be discovered as the new stars of stage and screen, but on the hunt for actors, movie stars especially, and their autographs. It wasn't long before my book was full to bursting with priceless signatures: Carole Landis, Victor Mature, Shirley Temple, Milton Berle, Donald O'Connor, the gorgeous Maria Montez, Mary Martin (who was soon to star in *One Touch of Venus*), Cornelia Otis Skinner, Alfred Lunt and Lynne Fontanne, and hundreds more. Not only during that neglected school year but also whenever I subsequently returned for brief visits with my mother, I spent as many days as I could in pursuit of names for my book.

My truancy would provide me with a number of interesting stories to tell, beyond just discovering places to hang out all day and all the weird people I met at stage doors or hotel alleys. Once, at the glamorous Sherry-Netherland Hotel, I was lucky to be picked to celebrate Peggy Ryan's birthday. She was costarring at that time with Donald O'Connor and Gloria Jean in a series of mediocre, cheap musicals. It was fun . . . especially to be photographed among such bright young Hollywood stars. Not too long after I met her, Peggy disappeared, not just from my world but from the public view altogether. How meaningless that early experience seems today . . . when reckoned alongside what I had missed out on in the classroom that day. Through all my years of teaching, I recalled my own poor excuses for missing school whenever a student told me of malfunctioning alarm clocks or pressing matters that prevented their attendance in my class.

Probably the most exciting, original thing that happened to me during my star-struck days, though, involved a thrilling experience that still I remember most vividly and retell whenever I can with relish and something approaching pride. I had been horsewhipped by one of the most important actors of his day, a man who proved himself a true genius as both an actor and a director: Orson Welles. I never tire of watching *Citizen Kane*, not the least for the opportunity of leaning over to a friend and telling them with great delight, "You know, *he* whipped me once." Of course, most of them refuse to believe me at first . . . but it is true. Orson Welles had just married the glamorous Rita Hayworth, who had already starred in *The Strawberry Blonde* and *You'll Never Get Rich*, as well as countless boys' (and probably girls') fantasies, thanks to those unforgettable photos in *Life* magazine. She was the strawberry redhead in the gallery of cinematic beauties. She was most beautiful . . . in fact, I would say she was more beautiful off-screen than on. They spent their honeymoon in the Sherry-Netherland, and we leeches, we autograph hunters, were there at the swirling doors each morning. We stayed all day, waiting for them to exit or make an elegant entrance.

One bright, sunny morning I looked up and over to Central Park, where one might rent a hansom cab drawn by a horse at the edge of the street and go for a pleasant spin through the park. As I looked over, I saw Welles and his lovely bride just mounting the first step of their cab. Stealthily, I rushed through the intersection despite the red light and crossed Fifth Avenue as the horse trotted up Central Park South. it was as though my short legs were motorized. I drew up to the cab and took hold of the door handle, forcing it to open. I trotted along, trying with my free hand to take my autograph book from my pocket along with a pencil for their signature. I was perplexed by what followed. Instead of accepting my pencil, Orson Welles reared up from the seat, grabbed the driver's whip, and proceeded to lash my flesh until I unhanded his cab and dropped away. For days the red welts refused to leave my back. But I had received his signature, even if not in writing. To prove to my cohorts that those slashes on my poor back were given to me by Orson Welles was difficult. They turned away from what they thought a lie. But it was the truth, even if I had nothing more than my word to back up my tale. I'm no masochist, but part of me laments that those welts have long disappeared into memory.

Ginny Simms, the Hollywood and radio singing personality, was headlining a stage production at the handsome Capitol Theatre on Broadway . . . I adored her. Only Veronica Lake held more firmly the strings to my foolish boy's heart. I managed to save up a few dimes and bought a corsage of camellias and had it sent it up to Ms. Simms's dressing room at the theater. It wasn't long before a call came to the stage door asking the person who brought the gift to come upstairs. I went, shaking in my socks. Ms. Simms was between shows, it was lunchtime, and she was having a sandwich and a coffee. She offered me some food after thanking me for the lovely gift. We chatted for a few moments and I was thrilled. She was stunning and gentle. She was intelligent and wise. To paraphrase, she said something to the point that she had granted me an interview as a favor to a young fan, but now I must grant her a favor in return. She made me swear that I would never be truant from school again and proceeded to explain all the reasons that truancy was not only wrong, but foolish, wasteful, and could lead to serious troubles both now and as an adult. I wasn't thinking of adulthood, though. I was thinking of my pain in that school, and of cold rain. I promised her I would never skip school again, that I would venture into Times Square only on Saturdays and only with approval of my mother. I promised her that I would concentrate on my studies and make up all the work I had missed. Well, I lied to Ginny Simms. Because I did not forgo truancy, nor forget autograph hunting in Times Square, and I did not make up the lost work.

When I arrived home that late afternoon . . . precisely at the time I was due back from school . . . my mother startled me as she sat at the kitchen table, having coffee and cookies with the truant officer. As I had done with Ginny Simms, I made earnest promises . . . and again failed to keep them. The next morning, a letter arrived from the juvenile court stating that I must appear on such-and-such a morning with my parents. I had missed more than two hundred days of the school year. My father went to court with me . . . by that time, he also was living and working in Bayonne, actually in the Brooklyn Navy Yard, building warships, now that the country had entered World War II. He was not impressed with my conduct to say the least. Nor was he impressed with my mother's assumption of her parental responsibilities. It was clear to him that I had become utterly undisciplined, obnoxious, a common criminal. I had not only skipped school but had also begun to both smoke and drink; I was twelve years old. He was very disappointed, hurt, angry . . . and somewhat feeling guilty for the part he played in the instability of these early years of my adolescence. But what I was thinking was very different . . . I had at last become like my childhood heroes, Rocco and Cigar. I was very proud and very pleased with myself. I had defied not only the teachers and my snooty cousin, but all of the authority in the world (I admit, I felt a twinge of guilt at defying Ginny Simms in the bargain but still managed to put that out of my mind). In my own way, I had peed onto the hard crust of snow wearing ragged knickers and smelling of garlic.

The juvenile court judge was kind and lenient. He said that I would serve six months in a reformatory. Still a Catholic, though weakening every day, I prayed to the Virgin Mother to save my skin. It was my father, though, who interceded, blessedly, fatherly, on my behalf. He asked the judge to suspend my sentence; my father would remove me from his wife's flimsy care and cart me home to northern New York and see to my well-being himself. The judge agreed, and a few days later, packed up in his Chevy, we took off with Anne McBride, the woman who would a few years later become my stepmother. I was never again to live for any length of time in my mother's house . . . visits, yes, but nothing more.

We went home north to Watertown, to the spring hawks, the eagles, and the robins. I was in time for the last few weeks of school . . . it had not yet let out for summer vacation. I was dropped back down a grade, which was probably for the best. Naturally, my lack of attendance ensured that I had failed all courses in Bayonne Junior High, even Latin, which I enjoyed. The principal of the school in Watertown and all of his teachers had been duly warned of my proclivity for truancy. If I was late to class by even a minute, they were to phone my father, and he would deal with me on that score. Needless to say, I failed to show the first morning. My aversion to school was at that time far stronger than my yearning to learn . . . a pattern that thankfully reversed itself for the last six decades of my life. I hid that first day in my cousin's house. Jewel Ortman was my father's cousin, but she and her husband, Harry, were also his best friends. They too had come across the border from Canada into the United States. When my father discovered what she and I had conspired to do, his anger was plentiful enough for the both of us. Even though her offense was seemingly a minor one, my father begrudged to his dying moment Jewel's trespass against his will and wishes in having given me sanctuary on that fateful morning. To her hundreds of pleadings he turned a deaf ear. They never spoke again, never again played euchre . . . in fact her name was not allowed to be spoken in his house. The next time Jewel saw his face he was lying in his casket. The thought of skipping school . . . or even a class . . . never entered my head again. I was clean, giving it up cold turkey. I was no longer a slave to that addiction. But I continued to smoke for decades until it nearly killed me. I gave up drinking for a while, too . . . starting again during the last couple of years of high school. Trying to be considered sophisticated among my friends, I would take a gin fizz or two, sweet and sickening. When I seriously started to drink, I went to vodka . . . straight on the rocks. That tale is still to be told.

I ended up doing pretty well in junior high school; I even passed algebra with a decent grade. I began enjoying school and learning, though there is a difference between the two. I disliked gym because of the instructor, but the other teachers were fine. I enjoyed high school even more and did very well, especially in Latin, English, history, and geography. Science and math, however, were a different matter. Without articulating a truly intellectual philosophy, I must have realized that I was bound to become an imaginative writer and that science and math would not be needed. I passed my science classes, albeit not with particularly flying colors.

Among my favorite teachers was Miss Marie, who had also become my voice coach outside of school. I emptied her trash, raked the autumn leaves from her yards, helped her plant spring flowers in the sidewalk gardens, and did whatever light chores she needed done in exchange for voice lessons. Hour after hour in her musty music room I stood at her piano and sang "Old Black Joe" and other gushy tunes. It was fun, and little did I realize she was simultaneously teaching me discipline, vocal range, enunciation, diction, and a love for the platform and podium. If I read poetry before an audience well today it is because of Miss Marie's instruction. Geometry was something different. I failed it three times. Poor Ms. Bell . . . she worked so hard to get me to contort my nonmathematical brain in such a way that I might pass geometry. Having already failed it twice, I failed again on my third try with a flat zero and never did pass it. I have proven to myself over and over again that I don't need geometry to be an imaginative writer, a poet . . . at least I have led myself to believe this convincingly.

As though she had just fallen out of a short story by Katherine Mansfield, Ms. Bell moved across the forefront of the classroom slowly. She was synonymous with quiet; she was gentle, lone, dedicated to silence. She wore no scent, nor makeup, except perhaps some white powder to scatter across a shining chin or cheek. Her dress was always plain, made from cloth of dark shades; her shoes, flat and simple. Her odd-shaped face was not round, nor square, but somewhat oblong, and her hair was barbered in a short, mannish cut. Her most outstanding feature to us students was her teeth, the upper ones being bucked. She wore glasses. I have always thought of the Dorothy Parker poem, that "Men seldom make passes / at girls who wear glasses." Ms. Bell was that girl. Her students were that man. We shied . . . always. No one ever offered to carry her books to class, nor to wash her blackboards after class. She was a complete loner, perhaps a typical teacher of those days: sensitive, good, but rather old-fashioned in her dress and her teaching methods. She was the type of woman who neither loved, nor hated, nor tolerated. She was just there doing her job as well as she was able, with little thanks from students . . . and probably not much from the principal either. She never missed a class. Exams were returned the day after they had been given. I can find no fault with her . . . yes, she offered a smile occasionally.

I remember the physical appearance of another teacher with much more clarity. My algebra teacher . . . let's call her Ms. Flynn, as she was fairly young then and might still exist in this world. She had been a friend of my eldest sister. They conspired against me. Not only was I the youngest child of my family, but my sister also feared the possibility that our father might take me, his only son, as his sole heir. In their various chitchats, Agnes would explain to Ms. Flynn that even though I had noble intentions of pursuing higher education after high school, I simply wasn't very bright. Ms. Flynn had me stay after school . . . she did not enjoy spending her precious time with students outside the classroom, but nevertheless claimed it was important that we speak about scholastic manners. As she sat at her desk, my attention was commanded by her large breasts resting comfortably on the desktop. My eyes bulged wide with distraction as she announced to me that while I was doing fairly well in her algebra class, it was not sufficient to get me into college. I was stunned. I was carrying an average of 90. She could not really know what she was talking about. I knew that in her flat manner, without smile or sympathy, she was telling me that I was not college material. I was struck with a brick, a baseball bat straight off the lot. I simply rose from my chair without a word, left the room, and promptly forgot all my observations regarding her breasts. Many days have passed when I have hoped that she not only knows that I have attended three colleges, taught at half a dozen others, and have earned a bachelor's and a master's degree, along with the honorary doctorate that was bestowed on me. At the risk of sounding petty, I even fleetingly thought of her unflinchingly judging words while being inducted into the New York State Writers Hall of Fame. I suppose that another person's low expectations of you can be at least as motivating as someone's exalted opinion, though I confess that the latter is still much more to my preference.

But we must now return to Ms. Bell. I took her geometry class in three successive semesters. I failed the final each time as I sat with pencil in hand and mathematical concepts in a chaotic storm inside my head. She was good, thoughtful, intelligent, and worked hard with me after school hours. I was in good stead in most of my other courses, but geometry? Forget it. Before we left the school for summer I was told to bring my father to the principal's office. He was not happy to lose a day's pay at work to attend school with me, but my father reluctantly marched up steps into the main office, distressed, if not necessarily angry. He took off his fedora, which he rarely did, placed it on his knee, and stared at Mr. Whatever-His-Name-Was, occasionally also casting hard stares at my profile. Obviously, I had done something bad or we wouldn't be here.

"Mr. Kenny," the principal opened. "I fear I have very bad news." I watched my father's stare intensify. "We have had news from his math teacher that he has proven very poor in his Geometry class. He has failed it for the third time with a zero. Not a single question answered correctly. His instructor was reluctant to speak concerning the boy." I saw his right fist gripping the brim of his hat and felt he was ready to fight, though whether it was with me, my teacher, my principal, or all of us was not clear. "Consulting with his other teachers . . . well, sir, we have decided that you must take him out of school. He can't be trained. He is . . . I'm sorry to say, sir, a moron."

I knew what was about to happen. My dad jumped up on his feet and was close enough to Mr. Whatever-His-Name-Was to give a solid sock to his chin, though he thankfully didn't. Instead, my father grabbed my arm and marched me out the office door. Another voice had been added to the chorus telling me that I wouldn't make it in the life of the mind. "Such, such were the joys . . . ," George Orwell wrote, quoting William Blake with irony as he recalled the literal and figurative lashings he received as a boy in boarding school. It turned out that my father's anger was not directed at me but at a school that saw a failure at geometry as a failure at life. For whatever reason, he knew there was more to me, to life, than vectors and theorems and he helped set me free to cast the line of my future into whatever pond might sustain it.

My life was not ruined . . . only stained. My wish is that Ms. Bell was happily relieved of her moronic students and rests comfortably. In her own right, Ms. Bell was a good, thoughtful woman. I know she genuinely meant well. She may not have taught me geometry, even during the many after-school hours. But she taught me dedication, especially in the face of repeated setbacks, and that the student—not the school, not the college, not the Board of Regents—always comes first. I hope she forgives not merely that my success invalidated her teacherly assessment of my potential, but also that I spoke of her teeth so rudely.

eight

Horses to Carry Me

There was a certain pleasure in high school. I had good friends, a very pretty girlfriend; we had lots of dances, basketball and football games, though rarely did I have the opportunity to attend the games. My weekends were frequently spent in New York City, where I was allegedly visiting my mother; more often, though I spent those days meandering through Manhattan and indulging in some of my old habits. When I did stay home, I did a lot of horseback riding. I loved horses more than anything in life. They were friends, family, a whirl out of the misery of life, or what I thought to be misery of life, or what I thought to be misery.

Symbol of freedom, of wildness, of mystery, symbol of beauty and grace, yet a beast of burden raised to pull the plows, the hay rakes, milk wagons, the hansom cabs of Central Park, the village buggies, the stagecoaches of the Pony Express. Ridden by whiskered cowpokes, bucktoothed Billy the Kid, the U.S. Cavalry out to spread death across all Indian Nations west of the Mississippi River and between the Mexican and Canadian borders. Stolen by the Comanche of the Southern Plains from the Spanish conquistadors, the horse became a noble beast to the Native American . . . an image of art; a symbol of warrior societies; a useful ally in the buffalo hunt that brought food, fur, and wealth to struggling Nations; a beast of ceremony; and, during the mid-through-late-1800s, a primary means of survival for the Native peoples of Oklahoma, the Dakotas, and elsewhere on the Great Plains. The horse . . . so powerful a symbol that when the locomotive first crossed the Far West, the Native people named it the "iron horse . . ." out of wonder and respect.

As I boy I loved horses . . . any horse: blind or crippled; thoroughbred or nag; living or dead; in a photograph, a painting, or sculpture; under my loins, in my memory, side by side as I curried its body, or as it chewed hay or oats. I especially loved horses when I sat in the saddle trotting, cantering, or galloping the high State Street hills outside Watertown. In those moments, I was free of all bondage, of angry rains, of loneliness, of Times Square weirdos and whips, of hateful teachers and cold classmates who refused their friendship. Horses released me. Most teenage boys where I lived took to the rowboat, motorboat, or canoe to swiftly ride waves down rapid rivers. I enjoyed boating, but never considered it a necessity. It was a way of whiling away a summer afternoon, halfheartedly fishing for trout that deliberately avoided your hook. Horseback riding was different. You were, first of all, one with the steed. Your figure meshed with its body to become like a kind of centaur: you had six legs and the horse had two heads. And you were both free to race the rains, to pass together the gray mornings of boyhood, the sun-drenched afternoons of youth. A horse understood your emotion, your passions, the hurts and disappointment, as well as the pleasure you knew on his broad back, fists clenched around his mane, knees buckling into his withers. Your small, thin body was no burden for his power; you were the weight of a wisp of wind. You, the young rider, knew his fatigue, his thirst, his need to wander through the ripe meadows. You knew his shod hoof, his frothy seat, his smell, even sometimes his discontent as he turned his head, snorting, prancing, and nudged your leg with his flared nostrils and bit lightly. The horse rarely patronized with false love. Never did he sidle up like a dog to lick your hand, or beg you to steal a bone or some raw chopped beef out of the refrigerator. If he followed after you in paddock or field, if he allowed you to stay saddled or to ride bareback, it was because the horse trusted and favored you, enjoyed your voice, smell, and the ride across the ridge or through a sweet clover meadow.

As much as I think I would have been okay with it, not all of my friends from that time were horses. My closest male friends with one exception did not attend the local public high school, but rather were enrolled at the Catholic school, Immaculate Heart Academy, from which my two older sisters had graduated and where I began my high school career before my father moved me to the public schools. Others, like Dick Paquin and Stuart Jones, attended high school in Copenhagen, some seven miles away from our homes. One of the friends I made at Immaculate Heart was Pete Hyde, and he found ways to lure me into trouble from the very first session of woodshop that we had together. We were horsing around, giggling over a penis-shaped piece of wood that we were assigned to carve into the fuselage of an airplane by Mr. Knapp, the shop teacher and also the school's athletics coach. Instead of doing our assigned work, Pete and I generally made a mess of things, and Mr. Knapp was not at all thrilled with our impertinence in his class. He threw us out, would not allow us to return, and flunked us to boot. That was fine by me as I hated carving anyway. I don't recall signing up for metal or print shop, but I ended up in them anyway, probably because all the boys eventually did. Ironically, Mr. Knapp's son Carl became something of a friend while I was willfully floundering under his father's tutelage. He was president of our class and also editor of the student paper. He announced one day that I was to be the student reporter, and that my duty would be to gather news (by which he meant gossip) for the paper, knowing both that I fancied myself a budding writer and that I was also something of a snoop. I was delighted.

My very best friend, though, was Joseph White, the son of French-Indian parents who originally hailed from Quebec. I could spend an eternity telling tales of my relationship with Joe: the nights and days we spent together, the girls we double-dated (mainly Sally and Caroline Kelly, with whom we would "neck" in the back seat of our cars); how we learned to drive on the "doodlebug" tractor that Joe's dad used on his farm's hay lots; the hours we jawed over our miseries regarding parents, girlfriends, school, going off to college, jobs. Joe worked in a drugstore as a soda jerk and I worked for my father, pumping gasoline at the station he had bought. Joe and I both loved riding the horses that were always around on the farm where Joe lived. Doug Longway owned that farm and he bought, sold, and traded horses . . . mostly draft horses, though occasionally a saddle horse poked its startled head from out of his horse van. Joe and I went through our growing pains together, and it was Joe's wise mother who gave us all the practical instruction we would need regarding sex, which mainly consisted of "always use a rubber before you get married." But as she believed we were both "good Catholic boys," we would assuredly abstain from sex until after a ring was safely and honorably placed upon a young woman's finger. Despite the backseat necking, we were both virgins throughout our high school days, I think. At least I know I was.

I had one problem that involved Joe. I was jealous. Not because he was better looking than I thought I was. Not because he was more popular. Not because he was better at math, or better at dancing than I was. Not because he was tall and I was short. Not because his parents stayed married and lived together until death did them part. Not because his mother was a better cook than my stepmother, nor because her nature was a bit sweeter than my stepmother, who was given to dark moods. I was a better horseman than Joe, I think because I loved both the horses' flesh and spirit more than he did. I was also a much better singer than Joe, who could not carry a tune. No, my jealousy was exclusively because of Jimmy Carr.

Jimmy came up from New Jersey to attend Immaculate Heart as a boarder. He and Joe were classmates there, whereas I had moved on to the public high school in Watertown. From eight to four they were together sharing classes, teachers, friends, lunch, rides, secrets to which I was not privy . . . and that galled me. Joe had been my friend throughout most of the year and we were rarely separated, especially over the summer. Many nights we shared the same bed in his father's house, or broke bread together at his table. There were few things that we did not share. Even now, I find it impossible to even consider the possibility that Joe shared his dreams with Jimmy like he did with me. Would Joe ever have confessed to Jimmy that he was positive he would die before reaching the age of thirty-six? And that I was his sole heir? I was to receive his books and his class ring if he was not married. I had told him that I believed I would not live past the age of thirty-six either, and that he would be my sole heir, receiving my books and my horse . . . presuming both that I had a horse at the time of my death and that I was not married. Somewhat out of keeping with our other prognostications, we were also quite sure that after college we would each marry brilliant, talented, and wealthy young women. Neither of us died at thirty-six, and only Joe married legally and raised children. He did marry a pretty young woman whose father, though not extravagantly wealthy, had some money, certainly more than Joe's father. To the best of my knowledge, Joe was a good husband, an excellent father, and a gentle grandfather, and he died a good Catholic. I was jealous of Joe's friendship with Jimmy, and I was jealous of Jimmy's wealthy background and family in New Jersey. Nevertheless, during our senior year, the four of us—Joe, Jimmy, Sherry Carr (no relation to Jimmy), and myself—would cruise down the public square, singing out our hearts to the pretty girls gliding along the street in their evening best, which at that time consisted of flared printed skirts and pretty blouses or dresses tightly belted around thin waists. My voice rang the loudest in the silly ditties, in part because I wanted to outshine both Joe and Jimmy. I must admit that Jimmy also had a decidedly good voice. The nuns at Immaculate Heart certainly thought so, constantly giving him plum roles in the school's musicals. I couldn't wait for the end of the school year, when Jimmy would return to New Jersey and I would have Joe all to myself. Well, all to myself with the exception of whichever young lady he was interested in at any given moment: Sally Kelly, Mary Jane Hughes, Katherine Bolton, and so on. As we passed the summer double-dating at the movies, going to dances, swimming at the lake, having picnics in the woods or eating out at diners, sitting on porches, or necking in our fathers' cars . . . there was no jealousy. Jimmy was safely ensconced in New Jersey and was no threat until after Labor Day, when the new school year began.

I can probably count on my fingers the number of occasions on which I spent time with Joe since high school. Why? I didn't see him for many years, more than forty, not since my own father died. Why? I had no desire to see him as an old man, probably bored with life, waiting for death in a porch rocking chair and counting the floating seeds of dandelions or flakes of snow piling up around his feet. I have had no desire to see any friends of my youth: not the Kelly girls, nor Sherry Carr; no Pete Hyde, nor Charles Major, who played a fleeting part in my life during junior high; not even Virginia, that sweet young girl with whom I was adoringly, foolishly in love with at thirteen. I have met with a few of them in passing through the years, but rarely and for only brief moments, usually not longer than is needed to say hello or good-bye.

My life has differed so very greatly from their lives . . . and not just because I chose to pursue a literary career, something far removed from their perhaps more common . . . if I may use that word without seeming to sneer (which is not my intention) . . . conventional, pedestrian, bourgeois lives that largely followed the rules, both stated and unstated, that were given to us. I doubt that Jimmy went any further with his singing than cruising the public square; Sherry went into the grocery business; all four Kelly girls—Sally, Caroline, Mary Jane, Camilla—got married, some well, some not so well. In Joe's case, he also chose to live an Anglo life; he was never as concerned with his mixed blood as I was. I was different. I was on the outside.

A gypsy woman foretold that I would hold books in my hands and her prediction came true, although I don't know whether she meant the books I would hold would be ones that I had written myself. I'm not sure what she would have predicted for Joe and the others, but I could conjecture that it would have been an a very average life filled with uncomplicated pleasures: presents under the Christmas tree, picnics on Lake Ontario, births and graduations and weddings, summer vacations in the Adirondacks or at Disney World or at Pioneer Village, bridal and baby showers, holiday cookouts, mowing the lawn, shoveling snow, working the same jobs all their lives, paying insurance, paying the mortgage, paying the installments on the new car they bought every three years, shopping in malls, eating at Burger King or Red Lobster, burying their dead, attending Mass, giving to the United Way, voting Republican, sending their sons to war if there was one, perhaps keeping a journal for the thoughts too uncomfortable to make public, always watching for good, clear weather, attending church bazaars and never forgetting to bring the macaroni-and-cheese dish, praising local police for doing a great job protecting them, attending a movie once in a while, repairing a grandchild's bike or fixing a leaky sink; certainly *never* being alone, *never* feeling lonely, *never* having fear or at least showing it, *never* taking on a new challenge, *never* facing the threats of life or the dangers that lurk out there in the world, *never* being wrong and always feeling secure about the choices they made.

The end of high school simply showed up without fanfare one hot June morning. Whether it was the end of the beginning or the beginning of the end, I was never sure. What it clearly indicated was that I was on my own with my own dreams and wishes, summer dreams and winter wishes. There would be no Joe to share them with . . . could he have accepted those dreams that began stealing into my nights as our school days were coming to a close? Joe was becoming a physical man . . . he shaved, he had hair on his chest, he had a steady girlfriend who would later become his fiancée and then his wife. He attended college briefly, but then dropped out and got a job in a local factory. He married, had children, grandchildren, but did he still dream of the things he told me about under the stars or side-by-side on horseback? I can't see how he still could have had the dreams I dreamt, least of all the nightmares that have always chased me through the dark nights like baying hounds closing in on their prey. Not that I think Joe didn't have dreams or nightmares . . . surely he did. But they must certainly have differed from mine as we have walked along decidedly different paths since our days of adolescent camaraderie.

I had time to tickle toes in a flowing stream; I had time to stop my hike and sniff the golden flower, the black-eyed Susan. I had time to while away a day, then a week, then a month, then a year on a beach in the Virgin Islands, guzzling cold beers under tropical palm trees. I had time to speak, to sing, to chant my words out to the world and to be violated over and over again. I had time to reconstruct my blood, my heritage, my family beyond my family. Joe was not concerned with any of that. He needed to feed his wife and kids; he needed to buy a new car for work; he needed to pay insurance and save money for two weeks of vacation down south. His dreams and nightmares were different. He stayed friends with Sherry and Katherine, with Sally and Caroline, with Jimmy and Mary Jane. He stayed in touch with the mundane, or what I think of as being the mundane, the corporeal, the Catholic way of life and the pursuit of whatever joy that life allows. Joe became composed and reverent, respectable and respected; he believed strongly in his work ethic and his family values; he was a dutiful son and a loving husband and father; he became a pillar of the community and probably a bore.

Though to the outside world I was shy and introverted, secretly I was willful and dared to ponder the violation of regulations; I lusted to travel and, most of all, I lusted to lust. I wanted big things and wanted to do big things. In my heart, I was uninhibited and longed painfully. I desperately craved to show the world, or at least my friends, that I was a revolutionary who could scar the world and time. I'd burn up the world as though in a bonfire, as though the world, and life, was merely a stack of cardboard boxes to which one could touch a single match and therewith set the heavens aflame. I would do, I would do . . . oh, I would do what none of my young friends would ever do—even Rocco and Cigar. Not Joe or Jimmy or even hellraising Pete.

Oh, Joe . . . I wonder what happened to you and your dreams? Was it that I had to live them for both of us?

nine

Alexandria Bay

After I graduated in June, I hitchhiked to Alexandria Bay, a summer tourist village on the St. Lawrence River facing out onto the famous Thousand Islands. Alex Bay, as the locals call it, was about two hours' drive from the Mohawk reservation at Akwesasne, though I dared not yet consider going there. The thought alone was intimidating. Through friends, I was given a garage in which to live that summer. I had a bed with a mattress, and the lady of the house, whose name I have forgotten, gave me some clean linen. Her husband gave me a job as a dishwasher in his restaurant, though it meant working well after midnight most nights. My larger goal for that summer was to become an active part of a summer repertory theater company that a man named Jack Harrington had founded with his mother's money. The Harringtons were a wealthy family from Canton, New York, and Jack himself had gone off to Broadway and played the male children in the long-running production of *Life With Father* until he was too old for any of the sons' roles. Still a handsome young man, he cajoled and coerced his mother into providing the funds with which to open the playhouse in Alex Bay. She would be the firm hand behind the venture: money, knowhow, the business smarts. His sister Pat would be one of his ingénues. The plan was for him to contract the other actors from among his acquaintances in New York City, and shortly thereafter college students would follow and take up the responsibilities of being apprentices.

Though I was not a college student, I did become one of the company's apprentices, much to my father's chagrin. He only barely tolerated my summer's plan, the absurd rationality with which I pursued my silly dream. I told him it was a pathway to writing. My father alternated between wary approval and disappointed remorse that summer. He came to see me once or twice and brought me a few dollar bills so that I would not starve. He did not approve of my dishwashing job, however. Nor did he approve of my living in a garage, which I had actually fixed up rather nicely, though it did get steaming hot every night as the sun went down and the light of the setting sun streamed in through its small windows. Although I ate very well at the restaurant and I was able to clean up my body there as well, I can understand why it didn't seem like a meaningful step toward either my dreams or my father's ambitions for me. He thought I wanted to be a journalist and to enter the School of Journalism at Syracuse University, but he also said I had no nose for news, that I was far too shy for such an extroverted career. In any case, I had no desire to be a newspaper reporter. I wanted to write creatively, though at that summer's beginning I wasn't sure if it was to write fiction or to transpose my fantasies and dreams into poetry. Acting in dramas was creative work, and some of the actors in the company also painted, sculpted, wrote novels or plays. This would be a step on the road to writing and publishing. I figured I would become a famous actor and, of course, I would make lots of money and have then the time and freedom to create stories or poems or plays, depending on what I wished. What an ideal arrangement! After all, my youthful dalliances in Times Square had shown me that fame came readily in the theater.

Not long after joining the company, Mrs. Harrington gave me a sort of limited squatter's rights to the playhouse. There was a cot in the theater as well as bathrooms, and since I also still had a job at the restaurant, there was no problem about where, what, or when to eat. She was generous, but her generosity had been severely overtaxed lately not only by her children, Jack and Pat, but by all of the surrogate children who comprised the theater company. She did not need more misery from me. The other apprentices, mostly wealthy college students, lived in hotels. My second night in the theater, I was sleeping in total darkness when I heard footsteps nearing my cot. I could see nothing. It was a sepulcher, a tomb, a coffin in a story by Poe. Terror began to grow in the pit of my stomach. The soft footsteps came closer to the cot. Fear welled in my guts, turning and knotting over and over until my innards felt like a twisted rope. I burned to yell, scream. But my tongue and vocal cords would not respond to my urgent and fearful demands to scream. But who would hear? The entire company had left the playhouse: Mrs. Harrington had gone back to Canton, while the older actors were either eating supper at the river café, quaffing a beer in one of the local bars, or nestled asleep in bed. I had no idea where the other two apprentices were, nor whether Jack and Pat were on the premises. I knew only the welling dread, the terror that someone or thing was about to slide a sharp blade into my flesh, or to blow off my head with a gun.

The footsteps ceased moving. The auditorium was totally and completely silent. No mouse scurried, no fly buzzed. The black of the room engulfed my trembling body. Then I began to smell it, the unmistakable scent of another human being, acrid and hot, yet moist and sweet at the same time. I could smell armpits and crotch, I could also smell grease paint and male sweat. At last I could move, finally my tongue could sputter and my vocal cords scream, if need be. An invisible figure was standing over me, and I edged to the far side of the cot, shaking and convinced that death was only a second away. I screamed loudly over and over until a hand reached out of the dark and covered my mouth.

"Don't scream. I am not here to hurt you. I promise I won't harm you. Don't scream and I will take my hand off your mouth. Promise."

A second hand moved in the black space above me and lowered itself to my groin, fondling my genitals. I lay absolutely still, quivering, shaking, absolutely terrified by this horror, this familiar nightmare.

"Don't scream. Be quiet. I won't hurt you. Relax."

I lay as though in death, rigid, frozen ice, a rock, stone.

The one hand arose from my mouth, while the other hand continued to fondle my genitals.

"Please. Please." Pitiful, agonized.

"Don't do that. Don't. Don't," I whispered.

"Please . . ." And a face moved down out of the dark and rested its sweaty, flushed cheek on my groin.

And with that I was back at Aunt Jennie's farm . . . out to look for my hound dog, Happy. I was racing through the woods just after passing the pigsty. A man was in the woods. He stood there with my hound on a rope . . . "You want to play a game?"

I screamed. The face shot up and away from my prone body. The hand that had fondled my genitals moved off as well. Three, four, five, six seconds later a flash of light lit up the auditorium. A door slammed.

In the morning Mrs. Harrington told me that I could no longer sleep in the theater because it was dangerous. I was a minor. She could not possibly be responsible for anything that might happen to me in a tourist town with all sorts of weird men walking the streets. After that I went back to sleeping in the restaurant owner's garage.

Nothing like that night's horrifying experience happened again while I was in Alex Bay. Mrs. Harrington made sure to hush things up. I was constantly, secretively on the lookout for clues that might reveal the identity of my abuser. There were numerous professional actors in the company. I stared them all down, and I listened intently to their voices every time they spoke lines while on stage either rehearsing or acting. I listened in restaurants, in the green room, in the dressing room, while boating on the river with various men. One day, one of the actors from the company invited me to go boating alone with him. It was him, I was sure. I said yes and went into the rowboat with him, unsure how I would prove my suspicions or what I would do in the event that I could. Nothing happened. I was wrong. It was not the same pleading voice from that black night. Despite some strong suspicions through the years, some of which have verged on certainty, I never discovered who this maniac was, the perpetrator of this heinous crime.

By summer's end, I had played a few bit parts like Oscar in *John Loves Mary*, and I had been the understudy for the male lead, the sleazy hustler, in *Ladies in Retirement*, which remains one of my favorite plays and films. My intention had become to strike out for New York City. You see, I had fallen in love with a pair of preciously gorgeous ingénues: Thalia and Melpomene. I had fallen in love, but it was not clear whether that love would be requited. You see, I was short and not particularly handsome, though on occasion I was told my face was cute. I was skinny and spoke with a pronounced northern New York accent, one with much too much hay and horsehair entwined amid my words. And I was very young. I wouldn't stand a chance at getting a part on Broadway . . . everyone in the company advised me to go to college instead: "Learn a trade. Go home and work for your father and pump gasoline. Forget the theater. You just don't have it, kid. Maybe in thirty years you can get character roles, but not now. You're what, eighteen . . . at most? Well, whatever you are, you *look* thirteen." And I did. But I had fallen in love, and what can you tell such a fool that they will listen to?

ten

Acting the Part

The night I left the Alex Bay Theater it rained, dark and somber. My father came to fetch me at the end of the season. He was quite perturbed to learn that I had saved some dollars and was hell-bent on leaving the very next morning for New York City. I had no place to stay. I knew no one, though my mother was still living in Bayonne, New Jersey. I could always show up at her door, if things went sour. It took some convincing, but he relented: "You can stay a year, and then I shall come for you." As it turned out, I stayed longer. He visited once.

The next morning I left town on a Greyhound bus, a steed I came to know and to love nearly as well as my beloved horses. It rained all the way into New York City. Angry, troubling rain that frightened and depressed me, making me doubt the sanity of the decision that had seemed so good just a few days earlier. My spirits were soggy. My hope low. The rain beat ferociously against the front windshield of the bus, which I could observe from my seat. It slashed diagonally against the window where I sat. A fellow passenger attempted conversation, but I was not interested in what the nice old lady had to say about her grandchildren . . . especially when she pulled out the plastic photo album filled with their grinning faces. I was disconsolate. Rain washed the bus clean, washed the road, washed the gullies along the road, made swamps of the fields we passed. As it had been years before in Syracuse, the rain was angry . . . and I was running away again. The skies thundered.

Like Jon Voight's character Joe in *Midnight Cowboy*, I stayed that night in the Hotel Claridge at Forty-Fourth and Broadway in Times Square. When I saw the movie years later, I laughed to think that both he and I were dishwashers moving to New York for work . . . the jobs we were seeking were decidedly different. The Claridge was an old stomping ground of mine from the autograph-hunting days, but I couldn't afford it for long, though; the next morning I found a cheap room on Park Avenue South.

The rain had stopped. Pavements were fossil-dry, as is often the case in late August. The city was crowded with sun and sultry. But it was not overbearingly hot for me. It was glorious. I was standing on Broadway in old New York . . . Manhattan, Times Square, surrounded by color and sounds, the music of traffic, blaring horns and feet shuffling by. Who knew to whom that pair of loafers or those high heels belonged? Perhaps Robert Taylor or Greta Garbo. The city wheeled with magic. The signs calling out the names of shows and movies burning high over the street, the Camel sign puffing out circles of smoke across the Square; the waterfalls over the Bond clothing store; the hot dog shops where they sold cold papaya and pineapple drinks . . . cheap and delicious, my personal "Recession Special" long before Gray's coined that phrase. Broadway and Seventh Avenue . . . the Palace Theatre, the Capitol up the street, the Booth on the side street. I was indeed in heaven.

By sheer luck and adventuring, I discovered the Actors' Exchange. For a few dollars a month you could have your mail collected, use the telephone to check in with agents, or simply sit around and talk shop, gossip over a coke or coffee with other aspirants. The Exchange had a bulletin board with two necessities of life for those in my condition: casting calls for plays and films and listings for needed roommates or apartments for rent. I paid my few dollars and instantly became an actor, nominally at least. The very first day I met Werner Klemperer, who lazily sat around the office smoking and talking in a thick European accent about a certain play he'd seen the night before, how dreadful the weather was, and . . . oh yes, how he must, *really* must make the agency rounds. This was long before *Hogan's Heroes* made him into a star. Shortly thereafter, I was informed that he was the son of the great German-born conductor Walter Klemperer. He had a way of upstaging everyone who entered and left the office. To the receptionist, I'm sure, he appeared as just another grating would-be star talking more of a game than he could actually play. But I thought he was wonderful, a real working actor, all spiffed up, suave in dress and hair.

On inquiring about rooms, the young woman at the desk announced that a David Forrest was looking to share a double bedroom, inexpensive . . . four dollars a week, no cooking, no bathroom in quarters, both bath and pay phone shared in the hall, a short walk or bus ride from Broadway. The room sounded terrific, exactly what I needed. I could eat out at delis or at the Horn and Hardart automat just up the street on Broadway from the Exchange. I phoned, but was disappointed to get no answer from the hall pay phone at Park Avenue South that was on the other end of the call. I had no sooner put the phone back into its cradle when the receptionist got my attention by nodding her head toward a short young man of twenty-one years, light blonde hair, a round moon-shaped shiny face, strong jaw, and long arms with a dancer's stride. There stood David Forrest in person. He was an actor presently out of work . . . "at liberty," as they say in the business . . . but he was expecting an Army Corps film job as soon as his agent could work a deal. Quizzically, David looked me up and down. He smiled at me, but it wasn't much more than a hesitant movement of his lips. He motioned to step outside into the corridor.

"Why did you run away?"

Before I could answer that I hadn't run away and that I was in New York with my father's approval, he asked, "How old are you? Fourteen, fifteen? Younger?"

It was difficult to convince him that I had turned eighteen a few days earlier, on August 16. I looked fourteen, with no body hair showing, no facial hair, not even peach fuzz on the chin. Nary a razor's scar on what was said to be a rosy cheek, but which wasn't rosy at all . . . no, rather fairly dark in tone, especially with my summer's tan. I offered my father's phone number and address and told David that he could call him collect to check me out. We shook hands and walked to his building, where he showed the beautiful room with double beds, double dressers, one closet to share, and the bath and phone in the hall. He said the only two problems with the place were the bar underneath that played the jukebox most of the night, and the aging libertine actress next door. She smoked up a storm, and when she ran out of cigarettes and booze, she would knock on our door any hour of the day or night. That was all fine with me, though. I liked the room, the price, the location, and I didn't mind sharing the bath. My dad would surely approve of that tony-sounding address at Park Avenue South and Thirty-Second Street, and I felt like I had achieved stardom on my first full day in NYC! I gave David eight dollars . . . my share of the rent for two weeks. He took me out and showed me a Greek restaurant that sold a strange plate of spaghetti and also a deli where we could purchase salads, beans, and baloney . . . staple foods for out-of-work actors trying not to become hunger artists. The deli sold a delicious macaroni and tomato goulash dish that I ate hundreds of times after work, sitting on the bed talking with David and with some of the many friends who stopped by often to see him.

I'd died and gone to heaven . . . again.

Not long after I moved in with him, David said to me, "The first thing we must do if you are going to be an actor is to clean up your speech. Your diction is dreadful; you speak like an old farmhand from the Midwest . . . or northern New York, wherever it is you're from. No one will cast you with that diction. Then we start reading plays, memorizing lines and such. If you don't know the great plays of Shakespeare, you are worthless. And read. Yes, you must read, read, and read more. Thomas Wolfe, *Look Homeward, Angel* and *The Web and the Rock*, for example." I was thrilled. This fairly handsome, fluffy blonde, wise, beautifully spoken young man would reshape me . . . and he did in many good, positive, helpful ways.

David was born three months before me in southern California . . . Los Angeles, as I recall. He had studied the dramatic arts at the Actors' Lab with Jessica Tandy and Hume Cronyn. Before he had turned sixteen, he had been given parts in a couple of musical films, including RKO's minor hit, *Sing Your Way Home*. He met many actors on the sets of these films who became friends. He did not, however, feel complete as an actor until he had made at least some small success on Broadway. His former mentor, Jessica Tandy, was starring on Broadway with the young Marlon Brando in Tennessee Williams's runaway hit, *A Streetcar Named Desire*, and this had fueled his desire to stride the boards somewhere on the Great White Way. He had left California for New York with a decent nest egg in his pocket, and we met only days after his own arrival. David had the luck to get a job as usher in the Midtown Theater on upper Broadway, a film house that screened art films, mainly European ones. A week after we began rooming together, though, he found a job as usher in one of the legitimate theaters on Broadway . . . a change that served both of us well. Not only did he make slightly more money (and could augment his regular pay with tips), but we were also able to see many Broadway shows on tickets that were given to him as part of his job. I saw Irra Petina in a huge musical extravaganza called *Song of Norway*; I saw *Born Yesterday* with Judy Holliday; and of course I saw the magnificent production of *Streetcar*, plus dozens of other memorable shows.

When David switched usher jobs, I was in line for his position at the Midtown and grabbed it instantly. I received fifteen dollars a week . . . plus a couple more dollars in tips if I was lucky. Some nights I would receive as much as forty-five cents, and if the theater was really busy with a hit film, I might make as much as $1.10. I wasn't getting rich, but it bought the hundreds of baloney sandwiches we ate and the little containers of macaroni goulash from the deli down the street. I usually walked home from work to save the fifteen-cent subway fare, and on any given night David would have brought friends home with him. *Lend an Ear* arrived in from Los Angeles while I lived with David and it opened as a tremendous hit on Broadway. David knew practically every actor, singer, and dancer in the show, including its stars: Carol Channing and Gene Nelson and Yvonne Adair. They may well have been sitting on my bed, talking shop along with Bob Scheerer or William Eythe. Some nights he would be conversing with Joan Loring, the actress who had achieved great prominence a few years earlier in the film *The Corn Is Green*. Thrill after thrill. I sat tongue-tied before these gods and goddesses of the art.

Speaking of goddesses, if I may be permitted a quick story off to the side. I wasn't telling the complete truth when I said the dramatic muses were the only loves I pursued down to the city . . . there was another less abstract object of my affection. She was the vivacious Midge Longley, an actress in the summertime company in Alex Bay. Midge was a graduate of St. Lawrence University. Always the amateur ham, the cutup, the scene-stealer, she had an abiding fascination for the stage. She had met Jack Harrington through his younger sister Pat, who had convinced her to audition for her brother's company. He hired her almost immediately. For the whole summer she was marvelous in her many roles; she was especially good in *Ladies in Retirement*, in which she played one of the wacky spinster sisters. I can visualize her now in costume and can't hold back my laughter. Elsa Lanchester had played the same part in the Hollywood film, which starred Ida Lupino. To me Midge was glamorous . . . I had no idea she was not a famous Broadway actress. I fell in love. I haunted her rehearsals. I never missed a performance. I was overjoyed to run for a glass of water or to fetch her forgotten script. I practically took up residence outside her dressing room and I mooned about behind her wherever she walked. After I moved to New York and she returned there after her summer up north, I camped pretty much on her doorstep whenever I could; she lived in a brownstone on the Upper West Side in New York City. It must be added here that Midge did not return my sentiments. She looked upon me as a confused kid brother, much as David did. She offered whatever succor she had to give, which most often meant nothing more than sharing slices of pizza on her brownstone's front stoop. It wasn't until nearly fifty years later that I had the pleasure of her company for dinner. We sat side by side . . . smirking almost wistful little "I know" gestures at each other's glistening eyes. She was still wonderful, magnanimous. I fell in love all over again. She was a most remarkable woman who ended up not doing much in the theater, but went on to do great things at the *New York Times* and with her own public relations company.

Anyway, my youthful paradise in David's apartment did not last forever. A young lady named Jan Folks lived upstairs from us in the rooming house. She was a costume designer, also originally from California. David and Jan met in the corridor of our house, and shortly thereafter, David was spending fewer nights in our room and more nights in hers. Several months later he announced that he and Jan were to be married and they would probably return to Los Angeles, where he could get work in Hollywood. Broadway proved to be his nemesis. No agent could book him. He found work in some U.S. Army Signal Corps films and picked up a handful of small, uncredited roles in movies that were filming in New York, like *City Across the River* (I, too, had a walk-on as an extra in *City* . . . I ran across a rooftop!). Bags packed, the married couple returned to sunny California. It was many years later during a visit to New York that I literally bumped into David on West Forty-Fifth Street, the heart of the theater district. We spoke briefly, but he didn't express much interest in my furthering my showbiz education. He wasn't working in either a play or film and he and Jan had divorced. I never saw David Forrest again, but for all these years I have looked minutely at each and every cast list of the films and plays I have seen. Never once have I seen his name listed, though.

David Forrest still had a major influence on my youth. He not only taught me how to speak and what to read, but also helped convince me that I was worthy of respect, that I was not a complete idiot. Even though I'm not sure he ever found them for himself, he also made me believe that one day I would know some success and happiness in my life and work. He knew full well that I would never be an actor, but perhaps I had some of the right stuff to be a writer, a poet. His support, approval, aid of various sorts . . . elocution lessons, informal therapy . . . were invaluable and perhaps helped save my mind and life; he certainly guided me through what otherwise might have been a maze and morass of dark confusion.

I remained in the city for just a little more than a full year, failing to catch a break in any part of the theater beyond the lobby. One day my father and my stepmother drove to the city and simply took me back to northern New York without much ceremony. I didn't have much money left and therefore couldn't offer much of a counterargument to their plan. My theatrical career had seemingly ended, not with a flourish but rather with Eliot's "whimper." I felt the heat of wanderlust nearly the entire time I was back in the North Country and, after slightly less than a year, I took off. I would not return to my father's house until 1956, nearly eight years later.

eleven

Hitchhiking

After I left my father's house, I returned for a brief spell to New York. Mr. Blythe, my manager, hired me back as an usher at the Midtown Theater. Mr. Blythe had been a burlesque clown when he was younger, though he liked to claim that he was a leading actor. He was a good man and treated me well, often buying me suppers at the drugstore across Broadway from the movie house or giving me subway fare so that I didn't need to walk. One day he confided in me that he was going to marry and would shortly thereafter leave his position as manager. He married the very young and pretty ticket-seller who worked at the Midtown. He was well into his fifties at the time, and she was still under thirty. They went off together . . . and in a short time I went as well, though not arm-in-arm with a pretty ticket-seller. Theater had proven it wasn't my forté. I couldn't act.

Many acquaintances, including David and Midge, attempted to sway me toward going to college, but I chose not to listen. Other friends spoke of the magic, the mystery, the beauty, and the inexpensive life one could know in Mexico. I fired up at that. I used to fire up easily. Fantasy overtook me. I put some dollars away, which wasn't easy, given my income of fifteen dollars. I could take the Greyhound to Richmond, Virginia, and from there I would hitchhike to the Mexican border and somehow cross the border. I hadn't the foggiest idea of what I was doing. But . . . Mexico! I would go and live, write great poems, and become rich and famous. After buying my bus ticket, I had thirty-nine dollars in my pocket when I left New York City.

In those years, Richmond was a sleepy small city, but my impression of it may well be clouded by years, or perhaps I've seen too many Civil War films. Even Atlanta . . . with its boiling hot Peachtree Street . . . seems now small in the long haze of memory. I wandered down Richmond's main street, inquired as to where the highway was so that I could commence my thumbing for a ride. After getting what felt like good information, I was off and walking, but I spent most of that hot summer afternoon with my thumb sticking up in the breezeless air. Somehow, I got myself to the state of North Carolina, and made a decision to go visit the house in Asheville in which Thomas Wolfe was born. Thanks to David, Wolfe had become something of an icon to me. His real and imagined sufferings as a writer, a teacher, and a lover while living in New York, trying to complete his novel, appealed to my sense of the tragic. I spent only a day in Asheville, a charming southern city in the Smoky Mountains, and was soon off and thumbing again. As luck would have it, a friendly gentleman offered a ride after only a few minutes. As we conversed, he recognized that I was from the North; he also figured out that I did not have much money and was taking something of an escape route from reality. Mexico would never have dented the skins of his imagination. He kindly offered me supper and a bed in his home. His wife welcomed me grandly into their house, as though I was a young man of importance. It proved a nice respite from a long stretch of uncomfortable days and nights on the road.

I traveled on through the hot weather and debilitating humidity of the South, which did not appear hospitable. I found myself standing on a roadside near the campus of the University of Alabama in Tuscaloosa. It was a sultry, starry night. My thumb in the air, a limousine squealed to a halt. In the front seat were two men, one young and dapper, the other middle-aged and moving toward portly. They assumed I was a college student . . . at least the older man did. They drove me into Montgomery, an hour or so down the road. The young college-boy driver eyed me through the rearview mirror with what seemed like some consternation and a certain hesitant doubt. I was pretty wild looking after a couple of weeks on the road . . . dirty, soiled clothes; my hair needing a good swipe with shears; my skin brown as a berry. Also, my northern accent gave me away . . . as something, though quite what I wasn't sure. He drove straight to the State Capitol Building, where the older man departed, saying to his driver, "Take this boy to the Western Corral for some chow. Give him some money, too." As he had been doing throughout the drive, the younger man gave him a prompt "yessir" and we went to a restaurant not far away.

The driver parked, but did not turn off the ignition. He slid over, leaned back, opened the door, and whispered, "Get out. You're a phony. You're no college student . . . not like Hizzoner thought you were. Boy, do you know who that was?" I certainly did not, other than knowing he had to be a man of wealth and power to take a limousine ride across the state. "Boy, don't you recognize that good man who offered you hospitality?" Even though Wolfe wrote about North Carolina, I felt like I was living in the middle of one of his novels. At that time, it wasn't much different from Alabama. "That was the lieutenant governor of the state of Alabama, boy. Now get out. And don't look back." I had heard similar lines in movies about the South and West. I knew what he was saying; there was a real threat behind his words. I did not have supper at that elegant restaurant, nor did the driver give me any of the money that his boss told him to. I hurried out of town as fast as my youthful legs and my thumb could get me . . . and, as instructed, I did not look back.

A tractor trailer zoomed down the road. My thumb in the night darkness, I was sure the truck driver would not see me, but I was wrong. He did. He pulled to a screeching halt a few yards down the black road. The driver opened the cab door and motioned for me to hop up and in. Instantly, I fell asleep, hardly giving him my name and destination, or hearing where the truck was headed. When I awoke I was on the outskirts of New Orleans. Amazingly, I still had nearly twenty-nine dollars on me. The driver was singing some western ditty about leaving Hilda back in the bar with another fella and how he would return and get her back. He told me to reach down on the cab floor, where I'd find a cup of coffee. He'd stopped only minutes ago, but I was asleep, so he hadn't woken me. The coffee was great. I hadn't eaten for what seemed like days, weeks . . . not since the generous North Carolinian family had fed me and given me a bed for the night. The driver didn't have much use for conversation, but I blabbered wildly about my travels down into the South, the experiences I'd had thus far, and where I was going. He frowned at the word Mexico as though I had said I was following Dante down into Hell.

After a while, we were in downtown New Orleans, on Canal Street where Tennessee Williams's streetcar plies the struggling surf of Louisiana's humanity. I stepped out of the truck's cab into a climate that was blatantly belligerent, like nothing I'd ever felt in New York. It was not hot. It was torrid. Oppressive. It was somehow massive. I found my way to the train station, not to buy a ticket but to make a temporary home out of a waiting-room bench, to gather my wits, and to make some decisions, the first of which was whether I would call my father and apprise him as to my whereabouts. Surely, he was worried. Then I'd need to find something to eat . . . southern fried chicken and cornbread . . . the latter, a staple food in my father's house . . . or traditional local food, red beans and rice, catfish? For the remainder of the day I leisurely strolled through the old French Quarter in total fascination. I ate some food, some kind of soup with white bread, and found a shop that sold pralines, the sweetest candy I have ever sunk a tooth into. I became ill. The sugar overpowered what by then had become an overly sensitive stomach.

I queasily returned to the train station, right in the heart of downtown New Orleans. I bided my time, summoning the courage to phone my father. Prolonging my confusion, I suppose. Someone suggested that there was a Western Union office on such-and-such street, just off Canal. The station is at the far end of Canal. I shall never understand the reasoning behind the route that I eventually took to get to a phone. Why, why I decided to walk to that office via a dim back alleyway, I cannot fathom. I didn't get halfway down the alley before three or four men stepped out of the shadows and jumped me. They beat me severely, but luckily, they broke no bones. They emptied my pockets of my twenty-nine dollars and took the contents of my little gym bag, which held not much: a bar of soap, a razor, a comb, a brush, toothpaste, a change of underwear, a fresh shirt, and two pairs of socks. I was left on the cement with a bloody nose and a tinge of luck that they hadn't done any worse by me.

The return to the train station was a walk of total humiliation and pain. My bleeding nose had dripped down my shirt. My face was puffy and my nose so sore that I dared not touch it, fearing it would unhinge and fall down into my palm. At the station, I cleaned myself up as best as I could in the grubby men's room sink. I spent the night on the bench without anyone else bothering me. Where were the city police, protecting the sanity and safety of the station from what had become bums like me? And I was a bum at that point . . . vagabond, vagrant, homeless, cashless, exhausted, terrified, lonely, and frightened beyond rational thought. I was soon to be twenty years old and appeared to the world as a most vulnerable fourteen . . . a boy who didn't yet shave and had no need of the razor those muggers stole along with everything else.

In the morning I returned to Canal Street, found a pay phone . . . borrowing a dime to make the long-distance call from a New Orleans cop, who stood by waiting to retrieve his coin as soon as the operator made the connection. I was grateful for his loan. Where was David? Where was Midge? Where were Rocco and Cigar? Where were those friends who had convinced me I should hitchhike to Mexico with their alluring tales? Where was my own head, intelligence, foresight, vision, common sense? I had no friends on whom to call, and I certainly had not used any common sense. I felt stupid, moronic, blind. And I could very well imagine what my father would say. I doubt he would have traveled to New Orleans to save my life yet again. Incredible, impossible even to consider he would be as wanton as I had been, to scurry down the Atlantic Coast to the Gulf of Mexico to redeem my scraggly, mutilated frame, festooned with rags and dried blood. The thoughts roaming through my mind as the operator continued to ring my father's home were incoherent in their despair. How could I confess my mistake to him? Surely, he would hang up the receiver in total disbelief. The operator rang and rang. No answer. She continued to ring. No answer. He was not home. What was I to do? He was always home. He never went anyplace. He was a businessman. And if he wasn't home, my stepmother Ann was always home.

"I'm very sorry, sir. But no one is answering. Should I keep trying?

"Oh yes, yes, yes." No answer.

I hung up the receiver and walked away from the phone. My starvation prowled Canal Street. How was I to eat? I noticed a police precinct and went in. I inquired at the front desk if the sergeant knew of any jobs I might get . . . washing dishes, mopping floors, carting whatever, running errands. He glared at me as though I were public enemy number one. "Get the hell out of my face, kid."

Canal Street was busy with pedestrians, shoppers. The street was peppered with bookshops, record shops, curiosity shops, newsstands, fruit stands, and—fortunately for me—several five-and-dime stores . . . Woolworth's, Newberry's, and the like. I wandered through the stores. In Woolworth's, I could smell the cooked food coming from the restaurant counter. I wandered past the lunchers; I just *knew* that someone would eventually take pity on a starving homeless lad, but no one did. I went back into the broiling hot street, so hot the pavement seemed to waver in the fiery air. I stopped at a corner, where a huge wastebasket stood, inviting me to take out a newspaper . . . probably the *New Orleans Times-Picayune*. I clutched it to my chest and returned to Woolworth's. On my prior jaunt up and down the aisles, I had noticed enormous chocolate bars spreading their beauty in wide and deep swaths on a fairly low counter. Hershey's finest milk chocolate, chocolate with almonds, and bitter chocolate. The almond one would serve nicely, I thought. I fingered the bars as though I couldn't make up my mind which I wanted to buy. I'd first pick up the bitter, then the milk, then finally the almond and then dropped each back into their proper spots on the counter, and then pretend to direct my attention elsewhere along the counter: bags of mint wafers . . . pink and white, jelly beans, toffees, and so on. I swung around, put the newspaper over the stacks of almond bars, and snatched back the paper with two large candy bars clutched beneath in shadow. As though I was leaving Montgomery, I walked away from the counter without looking behind me and casually made my exit from the store. God was with me . . . or at least Providence watched over me as I walked out to the street, where I ran as fast as I could on my weak and wobbly legs to the cooler air of the train station. I gobbled the two candy bars in what seemed seconds. Gyrating, itching with sugar, but with a head made slightly clearer by having dispelled hunger for a while, I made up my mind as to what to do: I would go find my sister Agnes and her husband John in Missouri. They were kin, blood, siblings. They had to take me in and give rest and food, perhaps also some direction and advice in the bargain.

twelve

"That's All Yer Worth"

My sin of theft behind me: the bloody nose, the bodily ache and emotional embarrassment of the beating and mugging, the loss of my meager possessions back on Canal Street. I forfeited the chance for more torture in New Orleans by climbing out of the summer hellfires to the highway heading north toward Jackson, Mississippi, all the way to my eldest sister's home and family near St. Louis. Agnes married John, the young man to whom my father had so vehemently objected back home, soon after he returned from his service as a sailor in World War II. The smoke and fire had been extinguished, the blood had been mopped up, and the guts had been sewn back into the innards of those brave young men who had survived those horrible, relentless battles. Now called Agnes Lamora, she and her husband moved with their first (and, for a brief time, only) daughter, Terry, to St. Louis, and shortly after that to the old frontier town of St. Charles, Missouri. I knew they were there, should I ever need them, and it sure seemed to me like that was precisely what had happened.

With empty pockets and an apple that I had lifted off a fruit stand, I stood with smudged face and dirty attire on the freeway, my thumb again extended upward in hopefulness. I was tired, not having slept that well in the train station. I stood in the broiling sun, though I certainly preferred sitting on the guy-wire fence . . . but what driver would stop for a lazy cur who would not even stand? Various summer birds flew through the air, semitropical weeds bloomed on the highway's shoulders, and automobiles zoomed past, totally ignoring this suffering lad who more than anything in life needed to escape this unwelcoming land of Louisiana, another legacy of the French colonies that I didn't much care for. Well, I really held no animosity toward the land; the earth was indeed beautiful and neither the cause of my anguish nor responsible for the beastly lack of hospitality that the humans of the area had shown my body. Car after car surged up the road like lightning striking the sky, the roar of their motors the quick, droning buzz of angry hornets.

Seven in the morning . . . eight in the morning . . . nine in the morning . . . and then somewhere between nine and ten, an old Chevy stopped two feet away from me. I had watched it slowly chugging along the highway. It was black, at least that was my best guess for the color hiding under a thick coat of dry mud. The driver had the doors locked, though his windows were open, which didn't make much sense. For a solid two minutes he stared at me from head to toe, and back up again from toe to head. Then he unlocked and threw open the door. He said nothing . . . not one word crossed his lips. I climbed in. The innards of the car smelled of fried chicken. The man himself carried the scent of bananas. Strange, I thought. He was nondescript and sat close, very close to the steering wheel, slightly hunched. It seemed, looking down at his feet, that his legs strained to reach the pedals. His head was topped with a ratty fedora, and he wore bibbed coveralls over a black-and-white checked shirt. His shoes were caked with the same mud as his car and a tiny scent of manure wafted up from the floorboard. He was a farmer, or possibly a sharecropper. Good. That meant he was safe.

I tried conversation, but my attempt was met with a wall, or at least a screen, of quiet insolence. His attitude clearly conveyed a message to me: "I don't give a shit what your name is, where you're from, where you're going, or anything else you might think I desire to know. I don't care to know anything about you at all, so you just sit there in the passenger seat and shut up."

After a few minutes of monologue on my part, I caught on to his attitude and remained quiet. After a number of miles, he suddenly turned off the highway onto a dirt road. Dust flared behind us. He accelerated, drove faster on this dirt road, much faster than he had on the highway. He was now in a hurry. We drove several miles and shortly came to a hamlet made up of little more than a few houses and a gas station. He pulled up to the gas station and asked the attendant to "fill 'er up." The attendant was a teenager and a black kid. I looked about. The folks wandering around, sitting on small verandahs, porches actually, on wood structured bungalows . . . most without curtains hanging in the windows . . . were also black. One elderly gentleman walked over to the window nearest where I sat in the car and stared me down. "Whatcha doin' there?" he asked. "Just out to catch a morning breeze?" As I made to answer, the old man turned and walked off.

The driver was soon back at the wheel. He had two bottles of soda pop. He offered me one. I think it was Orange Crush, or maybe wild grape or black cherry. Unimportant. Naturally, when he turned the key into the ignition, I had expected the driver to turn the car and wheel back around to the main highway. He did not, but instead continued through the hamlet on down the dirt road. Well, he obviously knows a circular shortcut back to the highway, I assumed.

On the contrary, we drove further and further down deep into woods. Bayou country. The woods were so unfamiliar, filled with trees of types I didn't recognize, and various grasses and wild blooms I did not know either. Here and there spots of sun fell of the land, but mostly we traveled under and within shadow. It was eerie to say the least. Downright frightening. What ghosts were out there under those trees, zombies camouflaged by leaves? What wild beasts were ready to pounce? What old reprobate, furious with life and the world, was there with a twenty-two waiting for strangers to happen down his posted road, waiting to shoot someone's head off? I had read some Erskine Caldwell and I had seen the movie *Gone with the Wind*. This was the South of the late 1940s. They didn't like strangers in these off-the-beaten-path parts. Hell, they hadn't particularly liked me in most of the on-the-beaten-path parts I'd been to. I assumed someone might be moonshining out here and certainly would not recommend that strangers take a leisurely drive through their territory. My driver said nothing as we wound our way further into the bayou. It seemed hours that we drove down that dirt road, but perhaps it was my fear and the mystery that caused the hands of my mental clock to revolve at such distorted speed.

He stopped the car and pulled the hand brake, but didn't turn off the ignition. He reached over to the glove compartment, pulled it open, and retrieved a pistol. I had been around guns, almost always rifles, all my life. My dad had been a hunter. We ate his game: rabbit, pheasant, deer, and so on . . . He taught me not to be afraid of rifles, but to understand that they can be dangerous. They kill at the slightest provocation. Don't play with guns. As I recalled my father's warning words, the man hunched back into his seat and pointed the pistol directly at me. And for the very first time spoke:

"Don't try anything funny. I'll shoot the shit out of ya if ya do."

I can only assume the gun was loaded, the trigger ready, and that my driver, doubling as my potential executioner, was willing and able to shoot me then and there. No response was offered through my lips. My vocal cords were not working. But my memory shot back to the theater in Alexandria Bay and that horrifying night in the dark house. I froze. Chills passed across my shoulders and down my spine. My stomach began to bump and burble. I knew I would retch up the apple that I had eaten that morning and the soda pop this maniac had given me only minutes before. I was terrified. He released the hand brake and rolled his car further along the downward sloping road. We had gone less than a mile when he pulled the old Chevy off the road onto a cutoff and we rolled into the woods, into absolute silence. Not a bird's chirp; not a stroke or waft of breeze or running water, babbling brook. Nothing but trees hanging over us.

The driver stopped the car and turned off the ignition. He pulled out the key and thrust it into the pocket of his coveralls. Still aiming the gun at my head, he opened the door and backed out of the car. Once out he stuck his head in it again and ordered:

"Get out. Now. Hurry up."

He pulled out a hemp rope from behind the driver's seat, strode off a foot or two from the car, the gun still on me, and motioned for me to walk down the path. I walked several yards, before he barked, "Stop here." He pushed me up against a tree. He turned me around and slammed me up against the trunk, and then proceeded to tie me to the trunk, the rope slightly above my waist . . . a sensation I had known before but couldn't recall at that moment. It is difficult to convey the horror, the black fear that pounded through my entire essence as I found myself yet again in the clutches of a sick, violent monster; my body trembled as if I were naked in a winter blizzard, my mind did loop-the-loops. My legs weakened, they would not stand straight. My arms went limp, even though they were securely tied by the rope to my side of the tree.

I wasn't a "me" to this madman but a "thing," little more than a body, a flesh entity to dispose of at his will or whim . . . when he had me secure, he stood back and just stared, as if calculating what part of my body, this young figure immobilized before him, he would first aim at and strike. Then he approached at a closer angle. He put the gun down. I could not see, but I could smell the scent of bananas on his clothes, and the smell of the fried chicken that had pervaded the car became overpowering. I could even sense the wild cherry soda on his mouth and tongue.

Happy, Happy, my hound dog, was howling in the woods. Oh Happy, come home, now. Don't make me chase you. Don't make me run after you into the woods. Come home, Happy. And a man stood there in the clearing of the woods. Happy was tied to a rope held in his hands. You want to play a game, son? Now don't tell anybody we did this. Don't tell your Uncle Frank or your father. They don't like this game. Then you can take your dog home: Happy.

He pressed up against me.

Anything but happy.

As his figure pressed against mine, his smell became me. Banana, fried chicken, wild cherry soda. His sweaty face so close to mine, his hair fallen and touching my cheek. It tickled my nose. I sneezed. He slapped me. I was sweating. He was sweating. He was taller than me. Rain drops, beads of sweat from his forehead, dripped onto my face.

"Shut up!" he bellowed. I had said nothing. Not a word came out of my mouth. My tongue was tied. I may well have mumbled something. I may have groaned, whimpered: "Don't. Please don't." I wanted to scream bloody murder, I wanted to scream until I was dead because I knew in a matter of moments I could be dead. My father would never find me here. Rocco and Cigar would never find me here. David and Midge would never be able to locate me. Joe would get lost himself seeking my corpse. Rocco, what the hell can I do? Cigar, I can't piss my way out of this, so teach me something else now . . . how to save my life and my body. I wanted to scream. I knew screaming would do no good. He wasn't about to untie and release me. He wasn't about to let me go free and unharmed.

Happy.

I could feel the tip of the gun resting against my head, poking into my sweaty hair. Only when I had to endure the agony of shingles, years later in British Columbia, have I again known and recognized such outrageous, unmitigated, unendurable, excruciating pain. Not even the pain of a heart attack can compare to it.

His weight sank against my backside, the gun at my head.

Shortly, it was over, though I knew he had taken hours in his violations. He untied the rope from around my naked body. I stood there with my trousers on the ground and my underpants at my ankles. Through reddened eyes, and through my tears, I could see him pulling up his pants. He had cleaned himself off with a few leaves. He motioned to the leaves on the tree above my head, pointing to them as if suggesting that I could likewise use them to clean myself. He walked nonchalantly back to the car, the gun now listlessly at his side. He placed the gun back into the glove compartment, storing it away for another day, another hour, another boy. He settled in his seat and turned on the ignition. He was going to leave me alive, but also alone in a strange world, a weird woods, a bayou in sweltering Louisiana. I hadn't died from the gun or his utter brutality, but I might die of starvation and exposure.

Without looking at me struggling to pull my clothes back onto my soiled body, he called: "Get in." I don't know why I did, but in hindsight I suppose I knew there weren't really any choices being offered to me at that moment. By the time we reached Jackson, it was dark. No traffic at all until we hit the city, and then only a little. Along the way, without stopping to park, he pulled out a paper bag . . . it held fried chicken. Hunks of fried chicken between fat slices of plain white bread. I couldn't eat. I had been nauseated for miles, certainly since the scene at the tree in the bayou. We drove through the center of the city, slowly enough for me to jump out of the car if I wanted, but my wobbly legs, my weak stomach, my aching head would not allow it. At the northern edge of the city he pulled over onto the shoulder, right over a gulch. He leaned over me. I was sure he was after the gun in the glove compartment again, but he opened the door and proceeded to push me out. I fell on my side against the ground. I felt something metal hit my face, and heard him say, "Here. That's all yer worth," before the car sped off down the highway. It took a moment before I located the metal object that he tossed at me. A coin, ironically now the only money I possessed. An American quarter, emblazoned with "In God We Trust," "E Pluribus Unum" and such. A U.S. two-bit piece. Twenty-five cents. And that's all I was worth. He was right. I was a worthless, useless, ragged bundle of nothing with less value than a bedraggled cat, stuffed into a grain bag and thrown into the Mississippi River to drown.

My own sins and the sins visited upon me had multiplied.

thirteen

Brutes

That night, standing at the road's edge in the dark, watching lights flicker and blink in the distance, I remembered my mother saying to me years ago that all men were brutes. Weak from both hunger and the atrocity committed against my flesh, my boyhood, my youth, I could clearly hear my mother's voice. I may have been in Louisiana in summer where I stood, but it was a New York winter in my mind's eye. Snow slowly fell onto the roofs of the houses, the ground, the rooftop of the car parked in the lot beyond my house, the windowsill outside my parents' bedroom, where I sat on the bed next to my mother. Her one arm was around my shoulder, and the index finger of her left hand was pointing out the window, down toward the parked car. *Men are brutes. See? That's your father in the car down there. He is with a woman.* And the snow continued to fall.

That memory, the pictures flashed across the memory of the angry rain in Syracuse, as she orphaned me out to the Onondaga family, her friends.

And that night late in the dark of the theater, a hand reaching out of the blackness to cover my screams. And I remembered the other hand, reaching down and covering my groin. And my voice, my pain, my anguish saying: "Please, please."

"Oh David, where were you? Daddy, why didn't you tell me? Mama, Mama, Mama. Mrs. White, there is so much more to it than just using a condom, believe me."

And the stand of trees behind Etta Zeller's garden where we boys, little tykes of four and five, Carl and Jack and the others, measured our penises under the plums. Was that, too, brutal, brutalizing each other? Or was it merely experimentation, curiosity?

My mother had convinced me men were brutes and I could find no contradiction.

I stood in the dark. The night was balmy and moist. It was on a highway just north of Jackson, Mississippi. I was nineteen, a quarter-blood Mohawk boy . . . short, skinny, but "cute" as the girls in high school would sometimes say, particularly the girls I liked and necked with in the backseat of Joe's car or the front seat of my father's car. We would park high on the hill overlooking my hometown, near the old cedar tree cemetery in which I would ride my horse. I would tie up the horse in the cemetery, pull up handfuls of grass to feed to him, and give him a shot of water from the canteen I always carried for us on such days. And I would amble to an old stone under the cedars and dream. Even if it should rain, the horse and I would stay on the hill under the cedars. He would chomp on the grass and I would dream of the good life I had in store and the great accomplishments that would be mine in life. How proud my dad would be! How proud Joe and Rocco would be of what I had become!

Instead, there I stood in the dark . . . a mutilated spirit, disgusting, smelling of filth and banana and fried chicken. I could still taste the soda pop from his mouth. I could hear Happy's whines and I could feel the man slam my body against the tree trunk. I stood there on the highway a violated spirit, a ravished body, my flesh smelling. Disgusting.

Many years later in New York at the Living Theatre on Fourteenth Street and Sixth Avenue I heard Julian Beck and Judith Malina shout out to the audience gathered in the theater that the human body is beautiful and that we should know no shame because of our nakedness. At that moment in the dark on the Mississippi highway, though, my body was not beautiful. It was ugly.

In the dreamlike, unreasoning flood of recollections that flashed through my vision on that dark and lonely roadside, perhaps the most odd was Etta Zeller's garden. The image was plum trees at the end of her garden, and she was handing me a bouquet to take home, a bouquet of gladiolus, veronica, verbena. Aunt Flo stood near. She offered me a book, leather bound, old but in mint condition. The night came down, embraced me, swallowed me. I was lost in its folds. I stood on the highway crying. Tears rolled down my cheeks. What would Etta and Aunt Flo say now.

"Hey kid, why are you crying?"

I could manage to see only the whites of his eyes, and a white collar circling what I supposed was his neck.

"Get down here . . . with me. They coming and they is mad, man. They is blazin'!"

A black man in a black suit with a white shirt lay against the rolling curve of the gulch. He held a plain cigar box in his fists and he told me a strange story when I climbed down the gulch to sit at the bottom with him.

I heard doors slamming hard, and I could hear angry voices coming from the blinking lights, much nearer than I initially realized: "We gotta kill that thief." Surely that wasn't me, was it? "Shoot 'im!"

The man's story was that he was an itinerant country preacher, an alleged reverend. He traveled around, spouting Christian sermons, reading the Bible, and passing a cigar box around for contributions in compensation for his good works and his good words to the poor, simple folks in the black communities of the rural South. That night, he had been sermonizing as the cigar box passed through a not terribly large congregation when a shot rang through the night: "Is that sumbitch in that meetin' hall? We're gon' string him up!" They were convinced he had been committing crimes all along the highway to Jackson. Obviously, a group of men were onto his scent. They had located him in a church just off this highway where only moments before I had been hitchhiking, trying to find my way to St. Louis. Now he was hiding in the gulch, his box pressed tightly to his chest, his torn Bible between his knees as he sat on the ground telling me his tale. We could hear the anger, the voices going further south and therefore further away. We stayed fairly quiet for an hour. Finally he announced that it was all over. He claimed that the people had forgiven him and returned to their shacks. God, too, had forgiven him his ragged ways. And now he must be off. He proceeded to amble up the gulch, clutching both his cigar box tinkling with coins and his Bible. In a few moments he had completely disappeared in the dark, leaving me to wonder whether my mind was trying to distract me from my suffering with scenes from Caldwell . . . or Faulkner . . . or Twain.

Feeling somewhat safer with this preacher hopefully departed for either heaven or hell, I returned to the road and stuck up my thumb as a car approached the intersection. The car's bright lights lit me up just before the car stopped. I looked in through the front windshield, hoping desperately to see a family or least a woman driver. Instead, it was an American serviceman, an army man. I think he was a staff sergeant.

"Hey kid, where are you going? I'm going far as Memphis."

He opened the door and I climbed in. Surely, an army man in the U.S. service of the government and the people would be a safe bet. I had resolved not to accept a ride from another lone man, but his uniform put me at ease, reminded me of my sister's husband and his goodness. I commenced talking to him, though of course I did not, would not, reveal the tale of what had happened to me in the bayou. We chatted pleasantly on the way to Memphis. He was young, perhaps twenty-five or twenty-seven, and had a pleasant, if not particularly memorable face. He was slender and sat up straight in his driver's seat, which made him appear in command, confident. He wore a wedding ring on his left hand and a very wide smile on his mouth.

After a number of denials on my part, he managed to get me to confess to being hungry . . . I was, in fact, starving, having vomited what little had been in my stomach back in the bayou. He said he knew of a roadside diner up ahead and we could chow down there. When I told him that I had no money . . . I did not mention the shameful quarter hidden in my pocket . . . he exclaimed, "How much does a bowl of soup cost?" He'd splurge, be my Dutch uncle. Not long thereafter, the diner appeared on the side of the road. We stopped, parked, and went in. At his insistence, we ordered burgers and fries to go with the bowl of soup he'd offered to buy for me. Oddly, it was corn chowder, an old Mohawk staple soup that I'd eaten many a time back in the North Country. We ate and talked and laughed at the waitress, who was new on the job and getting a hard time from a bunch of guys at another table. After our meal, we left, arranged ourselves once more in his car, and drove off.

The car drove on down the highway into the dark night. The soldier sang tunes I did not recognize, which must have helped to lull me to sleep. Suddenly, he pulled off the road, turned into a stand of thick-leaved trees, cut the motor, and said as plainly as anything: "Drop your pants, boy!" Happy was lost again . . . the theater was dark . . . the bayou smelled of fried chicken . . . the soup from the diner was pumping up out of my stomach. I sat bolt upright, shook my head for a moment before I realized where I was and that the man beside me had not actually become my next tormentor. The dream, though, put an end to the strange calm and cheer that I had felt since he picked me up, and I sank quietly, sullenly against the side window as the man looked over at me, then resumed singing his unfamiliar tunes, the car barreling down the highway through northern Mississippi and into Tennessee.

He dropped me off just on the other side of Memphis and pointed the direction to St. Louis. "Sorry I got to leave you in the rain, kid, but I got to get to the barracks. I'm more than a little on the late side." It wasn't just raining, it was pouring a flood of water down to the earth from the cloudy sky. I was drenched and miserable within seconds. The rain would wash away the sins upon my flesh . . . at least the smell of them that wouldn't leave my mind. I wanted to disrobe and allow the rain to cleanse me. I was on an open highway and, even though it was the middle of the night, the troopers would surely come by in their cars and arrest me. I stood in the rain. I stood in the rain. I just stood in the rain. The angry rain. And thought of Leo in Syracuse, how he hugged me when I finally found his house. And how he placed his oversized shirt around me after a hot bath. And the good soup he spooned into my mouth. He wasn't a brute, was he?

And it rained . . . angry and cold, bitter.

I had to leave this horrible South. My thumb was up. It never came down until a truck splashed up the road, its lights flashing onto the wet pavement. It stopped. I looked. It was a man and a woman and two small children. The woman was reading the Bible aloud to her family.

"Sorry, son, all we've got is the bed of this truck in the rain. But you are welcome to it. We're driving to St. Louis. You going that far, son?"

Despite the rain, I rested in the bed of the truck all the way into St. Louis, even managing to sleep fitfully for brief stretches of time in my exhausted state. I have no recollection of how long it took. I remember only the rain gushing down the whole time. I sat huddled in a cold pool in the corner of the truck's bed, but I was going to my sister's and I was traveling with a family this time. I must have felt safe because whatever dreams I had while huddled in that wet corner didn't trouble me.

I hopped out in downtown St. Louis, waving my thanks to the family as they moved on down the road. By then it was midmorning. I asked a woman walking in the streets on her lunch break about how to get to St. Charles and then walked from the center of St. Louis all the way there, about twenty or twenty-five miles. The police in St. Charles helped me locate the house where my sister and her husband lived. I rang the bell, while the police stayed in the car, keeping an eye out to see if my story checked out. Agnes opened the door.

"Yes?" she asked, looking at the spectacle standing on her porch.

I was not only soaked to the bone, I was not only filthy with dirt and abuse, but my hair was in my eyes, my shoes were a wreck, and through some untimely magic of nature, a scraggly beard had appeared on my chin, and I was about to collapse.

"John!" she called, nearly screaming. "John!"

He was at the door swiftly: "Get out of here! Go on!"

They had not recognized me; they could not see their brother under all the layers of hurt painted on by both the indifferent elements and by cruel humanity.

John had me in the tub within minutes, while Agnes put food on the table for me. She also told me that our father had only recently left their house to return home . . . she turned her eyes away as she clarified that it had been that very afternoon. That's where he was when I had tried to call him from New Orleans. Needless to say, they gave me good rest, good food, and a bed, all of which I would continue to get from them for nearly a year as I tried to find my way back to a sense of myself that was worth more than that pitiful quarter.

I found a job carhopping in St. Louis at the Parkview Restaurant. My boss, Jack, liked me and eventually transferred me, along with another guy, to the Parkview's sister restaurant in Indianapolis, Indiana. It wasn't long before I was making friends and even had some money in my jeans that didn't make me burn with shame and anger.

fourteen

Portrait of a Student

It rained a great deal that year in St. Louis. It rained just as often in Indianapolis, but I stuck it out and remained at the Indiana branch of the Parkview until fall. I rented a sleeping room with the family of one of the cashiers. At the start of the fall semester, I enrolled at Butler University, deciding that chasing the relative abstractions of the theater or of Mexico had not brought me much in the way of success or contentment. Even after I started school I continued renting a room from the same family, until one night in the late fall, when I brought home a fellow student, a young black man from Trinidad. He was a good student, a sharp writer, and a very fine fellow who spoke in a fetching Trinidadian accent, colorful, flavorful, and yet suave. Birdi was a good person. We had been talking about writing poetry and weren't done with our conversation, so he had walked back to my house with me. Thinking nothing of it, I invited him in and he stayed only for another fifteen minutes before our chat was done, and then he left. The next morning, the couple that owned the house stood at the front door as I was leaving for classes.

"We can't have that here," he pronounced.

"We have a baby girl," she added.

"You will need to find someplace else . . . ," he said.

"Today," she added, bluntly driving home their disapproving point.

And I did find someplace else, uninterested in staying another minute. I took up residence with the Davidson family and ended up living in their hospitable house in Indianapolis for most of my years at Butler. Mr. Davidson was a lawyer and Mrs. Davidson the manager of a dress shop, and they had one daughter who was enrolled at Indiana University and married to a journalism major there. They were beautiful people, like another set of parents to me. For doing chores about the house, they fed me often and asked only a small rent. During my first year in their house, I had a roommate in the bedroom and study that were allotted to me. Bill was then a pharmacy major at Butler, though he had been a divinity student at a different college before. Bill was an okay guy in many ways; he read the Bible constantly and often out loud and in my direction, as though sermonizing me indirectly. But we also played Honeymoon Bridge most nights before going to bed, with the loser obliged to buy breakfast at the school cafeteria in the morning. Fortunately for me, I usually won. The next year, the Davidsons told Bill that there was no longer room for two additional grown men in their house . . . I think perhaps his Bible-reading had become a bit grating to them as well. Whatever it was, I had the quarters by myself from that point onward. I got a job at the Haag's drugstore downtown and sold sundries when I wasn't in class or studying. Life was beginning to show some sunshine.

College was something else. Why had I avoided it? I adored it. I adored my books, my study, my instructors, and my university. I studied hard, burned gallons of the midnight oil. After an initial year of getting my bearings and making a few missteps, I received pretty good grades . . . mostly A's, actually. I didn't miss David and Midge anymore. I forgot about Joe. I didn't need Rocco and Cigar . . . they had slowly drifted out of my thoughts, replaced with the things I was reading and writing about.

Youth was ebbing. I was broadening . . . mentally, intellectually, creatively. I signed up for writing courses; I signed up for poetry and drama courses. I reveled in literature. I read books all night. I was growing. I was getting too big for my clothes and I was shaving the fuzz on my chin. I was shy by nature, but now I became stoic. I had read my Emily Brontë, but I was Mohawk, too. The history courses offered in the catalogue did not cover the complete history of America. Little or no reference to Native Americans, nor the conflicts after contact with the Europeans. It didn't have much to say about African Americans either. I was greatly disappointed. I would need to study Native history on my own, as I eventually did. But I loved college, university life. I made friends, but basically those were either fellow writing students or some frat boys who took me in because I was smart. They would feed me and ask for tutorial help with their assignments, especially composition papers. I wouldn't be surprised if a few frat houses at Butler still had some of my papers in their files.

I was fortunate to have a range of instructors with divergent approaches and perspectives to the interrelated crafts of reading and writing. I took every literature and writing course offered, even advanced composition, although my idiosyncratic spelling and syntax presented great problems to even the most patient of teachers. My syntax was nurtured to some degree of health by Carey Graham's exertions, but my spelling has remained inconsistent and doubtful to a shameful degree, as woebegone collaborators and editors through the years will surely attest. I took a course on modern fiction with the incredible and unforgettable professor Allegra Stewart. She was obviously wealthy and walked into our class on Saturday at eight in the morning dripping diamonds and wearing a mink coat that hung down to her leather-shod toes. Stewart was a scholar of Gertrude Stein and led me not only to her but also to James Joyce, D. H. Lawrence, Truman Capote, and Willard Motley. She also importantly rekindled my interest in Faulkner. All of those novelists have remained not merely on my bookshelf, but in the light of my mind ever since.

I signed up for a course in modern poetry taught by the poet Roy Marz, a good man, an intelligent mind, and a lecturer of critical astuteness. He brought my attention to Gerard Manley Hopkins, Edward Arlington Robinson, and Robinson Jeffers. Marz paid scant attention to Carl Sandburg, Kenneth Fearing, or William Carlos Williams. The only women poets he taught were Amy Lowell and Gertrude Stein, neither of whom he greatly admired, a position that obviously did not endear him to Allegra Stewart. He favored the more religious or divine . . . though not necessarily mystical . . . poets, especially Hopkins and Eliot. That was fine with me. At the time I was having a bout with spirituality, trying to determine what faith, if any, I felt drawn toward. Not just Wordsworth's style, but also his pantheism was appealing and seemed very credible to my widening mind.

I guess one might say Roy Marz was a classicist. His own devotional poems were often written in sonnet form. We young student-writers hunted down his poems in various magazines, especially in *Poetry*, in which he was often published. I knew instantly upon reading Marz's poems that he would see little worth in my juvenile work. Accordingly, I was neither surprised nor particularly dismayed when he found small merit in my poems, even though he did not bite the tongue or spare the red pen in his critical remarks. I was lucky to place a poem or two in the English department's literary magazine, *Mss.*, which also published several essays I had written for Dr. Graham's composition course. Marz read both, naturally; I believe he was faculty advisor to the journal. I managed to persuade the jury of student editors to print a poem concerning the life and death of Dylan Thomas, whom I considered the most magical lyric poet of his day. Thomas was a poet to whose work I easily took . . . or was it his rather besotted and impoverished lifestyle? Most students are poor, and most enjoy a cheap bottle of Chianti when extra coins jingle in their pockets . . . and I certainly was no exception. I have never allowed the Thomas poems to be reprinted and can't imagine doing so; like the other silly poems I was publishing at that time in the Indianapolis newspapers, they were juvenilia, exercises in learning how to use a voice that heretofore had tended to shout or to stammer. These poems were written in a style that today might appear to have been influenced by Charles Olson's projective verse, but honestly, in the early fifties I had never heard of Olson or his Black Mountain School.

I timidly complained to my friends concerning Marz's sharp criticism of my poems. One close buddy in particular, the late Robert Petty, advised I that ship my poems out to a well-regarded author for a second opinion. I chose John Crowe Ransom, probably because he was at that time the editor of the prestigious *Kenyon Review*. I trusted Bob Petty implicitly. He not only was a very fine poet, and a student editor of *Mss.*, but also seemed to win all the poetry prizes at Butler. This fact pricked my literary sensibilities . . . though I liked him, I didn't think he was that great a poet . . . but it did not interfere with our friendship. Bob, a botany major, had had serious abdominal problems that bedded him in hospital for lengthy periods. We were close and took many hikes together when we weren't on campus. We shared pleasures of high grades and mutually relished contact with our various instructors on campus. We also occasionally offered each other the succor of strong shoulders on which to lean when things did not go well. Therefore, I took Bob's advice and sent a batch of poems to Ransom. I can't recall a worse defeat.

Had I listened all those years ago to Ransom's evaluations of my work, I would never have produced another line of verse, much less more than two dozen collections of poetry, prose, and fiction. Ransom was obviously a fine, if also minor, American poet; he had an ear for European classical forms and a restricted sense of rhythm that privileged such classical and neoclassical forebears. My successful rhythms do not hearken back to Milton and Donne, or even Longfellow (Heaven help me if I find his "Hiawatha" among my words . . .). I still find it hard to believe that Ransom would allow even Whitman a place in his canon, and possibly not Robinson Jeffers either. He would surely discount or ignore the rhythms of contemporary poets like Amiri Baraka, Allen Ginsberg, Jerome Rothenberg, and I dare say he'd turn away from considering the brilliances of Diane Wakoski, Susan Howe, or Audre Lorde. I don't mean to place my work from that time among theirs, but it shared their fate in never standing a chance with the esteemed critic.

It wasn't as though I'd been thoroughly rejected by everyone else, after all. In our huddles in the student union—really little more than a routine cafeteria—my fellow student-poets had shown some favorable response to my work. This group included Jack, an outright Eliot snob, and two graduate students specializing in literature. Werner Beyer had given my writing his solid approval, as had Carey Graham (who had humorously nicknamed me "Young Charlie Lamb"). I had even been oddly comforted by Roy Marz's simple but firm suggestion that I stick with prose. With the combination of naïveté and egotism that a young poet absolutely needs to keep going in a world that is increasingly deaf to the songs he sings, I was positive that I was the new Walt Whitman . . . or possibly even Whitman reborn in the America of the 1950s. Surely, Whitman possessed pronounced rhythms. Had Ransom never read out loud "When Lilacs Last in the Dooryard Bloomed," or "Out of the Cradle Endlessly Rocking," or even "O Captain! My Captain!"? Had he never enjoyed the symphonies of Poe, Hopkins, or Thomas, all of whose music, rhythms, I savored, relished, and wished to imitate. How could this august man, an editor and poet no less, be so cruel, so heartless, as to destroy the rearing, vibrant spirit of a young writer? Surely, Rilke would never have been so brutal, nor would William Carlos Williams have carelessly tossed off such a phrase designed to wreak such havoc within the imagination and soul of a burgeoning poet.

Even if Marz or Ransom were correct in their unimpressed evaluations of the poems I was composing as a student at Butler, I felt then, and know now, my burning need to write, to express my feeling to record events and ideas, to satisfy my hunger for a brother-in-pen. I bled my heart into poems, whether or not they were technically skillful. Being a thousand miles away from my father back in Watertown caused me to develop a dire need for a voice with which to sing in verse. I did not sing well yet with that voice, but surely Marz or Ransom must have seen *some* raw (perhaps bloody) talent. Marz had even mildly praised the essays I had published in *Mss.*, and he had liked the drafts I showed him of a novella I was then writing for Beyer's fiction workshop.

As it turned out, Werner Beyer was my real mentor, the second opinion that I needed and didn't get from Ransom. I practically forced this generous instructor, a Keats and Coleridge scholar, to become my big brother or my second father. I've never broken this habit of seeking kinship and have found . . . some of them might say imposed . . . it with many of the men who have come into my life. Being the only boy among three children certainly caused me to value a father figure, particularly one who could understand and support a young writer better than my biological father. I wrote few poems for Dr. Beyer. I was somewhat terrified of his rarefied position as the author of *Keats and the Daemon King*. As brilliant a man as Roy Marz, Beyer dealt with the truly classic while Marz taught modern and contemporary literature. I took numerous classes under Beyer's tutelage: a full-year survey of world literature, Romantic poetry and prose, two writing workshops. He challenged every word or mark of punctuation that I ever dropped onto a sheet of paper, whether in a creative composition, a classroom exercise, or a term paper. I hoed the row he showed to me, and it proved beneficial.

Beyer did offer rewards, such as the spaghetti suppers that his young wife, Ruth, prepared for his Writers' Workshop students (all four of us that he allowed into the class) at his home. He also occasionally passed along tickets to the Indianapolis Symphony, which I couldn't possibly afford from my meager drugstore clerk's wages. More important to me than these material rewards, though, were the strong support, the badly needed praise, and the sensible, strong critiques that he offered to me in response to everything I wrote. I deeply desired to please him and worked extra-hard to move the C that I earned on the first paper I gave him up to an A. More to the point, I wanted to receive his commendation on my creative output, the stories and the novella on which I was working. When I got it, though, it proved daunting. He suggested I send the novella to Houghton Mifflin, who offered an annual prize of cash and publication to the author of the best original manuscript submitted during the year. I turned to stone, a cold-footed coward. I didn't send the manuscript . . . in fact I didn't even finish the novella.

A few years later in New York, I met one of the winners of that $10,000 prize, Edward Hoagland, who went on to great success and honors as both novelist and journalist. I lived at that time in a building on the corner of Bleecker and Lafayette in which he rented a studio apartment and we ran into each other in the building's entryway. I was impressed with his writing skills and renown. He'd been reviewed in the *New York Times*. I, too, was by that time published. The *Watertown Daily Times* had privately printed my book, *The Hopeless Kill*, and a new Beat press, Troubador, had published *Dead Letters Sent*. Troubador was to be the competition for and East Coast counterpart to San Francisco's City Lights Books. I gave Ed a copy of *Dead Letters Sent*, and he in return had some pleasant words to offer regarding several of the poems. He was then teaching at the New School, even though he spoke with a pronounced stutter that sometimes made understanding him difficult. We had some healthy chats on various subjects, especially animals. When he had been very young, he had worked in a circus with the traveling, caged animals, especially the cats. I enjoyed his apparent confidence, which his stutter in no way undermined. Once he moved out of the building a few months later, I never saw him again. People have that way . . . they come and go, shutting doors behind them. Oh, the friends and acquaintances I've lost this way . . . to my regret.

After a long life as a writer, an editor, and an instructor of creative writing, I can look through poems and stories sent to me or scan a classroom full of upturned faces and touch with my sight the endangered, desperate poet, fully realizing the pain and disappointment that they are feeling as they wait for their first turn in the literary world. The first rejection note may collapse their sense of security, which most likely took years to build. They may already have endured their family, friends, and teachers, not merely frowning at their literary ambitions, but shaking their heads, advising the pursuit of law, medicine, business, criminal justice . . . or pumping gasoline. I have an all-embracing empathy for the novice poet who sits on the limb of an oak tree while terrible monsters saw at the limb. True, not everyone is a writer. It is *not* true that there is a book in each and every one of us. The writerly sensibility enters at birth and is directed over childhood by the many life forces around us, culminating in the sheer love of writing, a total fascination, a volcanic eruption of images and ideas. Poets are not just born, they are also made. To paraphrase Percy Shelley, "Life hurts you into writing poetry." It was Roy Marz who insisted to me that every creative person has suffered the slings and arrows of misfortune, that the artist *must* suffer. Well, believe you me, I jumped onto that wagon early and fast. I would walk down the streets of Indianapolis hoping that passersby would recognize the pain chiseled into my face. I supposed my countenance to be sober and somber, mute and mysterious, its brow and cheek creased from the misfortunes of life. My eyes downcast, my shoulders bent, I walked with an amble as if my legs could not carry the burden another step further. And I was only twenty-two. Mine was not a pose . . . I had certainly earned my right to express suffering . . . but neither was it a full-fledged craft. Finding that would still require considerably more time and help.

The end of a semester, a year . . . my last at Butler. I had taken every single course Dr. Beyer had taught over my years there . . . and he taught quite a few. At our last meeting, he said to me that he had believed there was a weed sprouting up in his classroom some years before. However, on that day he confessed that he had been mistaken. That weed was really a flower, a rose blooming. He said he had taught me all he had to teach and suggested that perhaps I should enter Northwestern University in Chicago, or maybe even Columbia, where he had studied under Mark Van Doren. He shook my hand and we parted ways.

Though I'm sure now that he intended these words to lift me up, I couldn't hear them as such then. Why had I seemed such a weed to him? Why did I need to go on for yet more teaching? Why couldn't I just start writing now? I went home to my apartment, which I shared with another student-poet, drank as much wine as I could afford to buy, and downed as many as I could of the various pills that stood so invitingly on the medicine-chest shelf. My defeat was complete. Misunderstanding Beyer and hearing too much of Marz and Ransom in my head, I walked for the first time . . . though not the last . . . into the realm of confused reaction. I was completely disempowered, to use a contemporary (and rather hackneyed) word.

I remember sirens. I remember tubes being forced into my mouth. I remember a policeman or a hospital guard standing over me as I was strapped to a cot on wheels, and his voice echoing over and over, "You don't have to go to the bathroom . . . shut up." And then I felt his flashlight strike my bloated belly. I heard a scream. What I remember next is sitting up in a bed within the confines of a large, dim ward. An African American man sat beside me. He uttered not a single word, but the warmth, concern, and kindness radiating from his eyes spoke of safety. Terror gripped me. Where was I? I shriveled in fear. Not fear of the young man sitting at my bedside, combing my hair over and over again, but fear of the abstract, the unknown, forgotten. Startled, I attempted to rise, but the young man very gently held me down, my head against the pillow. He continued to comb my hair. I fell asleep. When I awoke next, another young man dressed all in white was seated beside me on the bed. The black man had disappeared into the dim shadows of the huge ward. It was night. It always seemed to be night there; the few days—though it may have been weeks, it may have been months—during which I was there were always dim, and I was conscious of little but shadows. This man in white was an inquisitor, albeit not a particularly grand one. I cannot remember his questions, nor my answers. He told me I was temporarily registered in the mental ward of an Indianapolis hospital and that he was there to help me. I remember peppery tears moving down my cheeks. He spoke fairly softly but adamantly, and the words he pronounced were firm. Yet all I recall was a nurse telling me that someone named "Bob" and another someone named "Werner" had phoned.

There is no recollection of time, only dimness and shadows. Human zombies paced the ward, with cigarettes dangling from their lips, conducting music only they heard in the air with their fingers. The young black man rarely left my side and never ceased combing my hair. If I went to the bathroom he followed. If I was called from the ward, he followed me to the locked door. If a nurse, or guard, or physician came to my bed, he was always there, the comb in his right hand, the smile of safety and security always on his lips, muscles flexed as weapons should I need his strength, his defense. I never knew his name. I never asked, and he never offered to speak, to tell me.

Early one evening—I think it was evening—I awoke from a medically induced nap to find the black man rigid at the foot of the bed, guarding me intently. Another man in white stood near my head, which was down on the pillow. Next to him stood my brother-in-law, my younger sister's husband. He appeared worried. Tears were in his eyes. When I recognized Pat, I fell into sobs. The man in white asked, did I know this stranger? Naturally, I did, but was amazed how he knew I was incarcerated in that ward. Pat revealed that my father had sent him to Indiana to bring me home. What relief! I stopped crying. He bent down and hugged me . . . even though so many would have had me believe that men do not hug, nor cry, nor feel. He lifted me off the bed. My street clothes were at the bottom of the bed, and Pat aided me in dressing. At the door of the ward I turned to say good-bye to my friend, companion, and guardian. Naturally, he was there, watching me depart. The comb was now in his shirt pocket. I think it was red. I can't for sure describe the emotion I saw in his eyes and on his lips, but it seemed that a door had closed on his life and that the world had stopped. I looked as deeply as possible into the black pools of his eyes and thanked him with all my heart. He had probably saved my sanity. I could not give him a single word or sound of gratitude. I reached out my hand to touch his shoulder, but he wrenched back. As Pat and I hurriedly reeled through the doorway, I heard my comrade say, "Thank you. Good-bye."

Outside I found my sister Mary waiting with a container of medicine held tightly in her grasp. She was pale and as frightened as I was. "A Dr. Beyer called Daddy," is all she said. All the way home to my father's house in Watertown, that was the only expression Mary uttered: "Dr. Beyer called Daddy."

It was a quiet trip across an ominously black night.

There is, of course, no way I would ever dream of accusing John Crowe Ransom or Roy Marz or Werner Beyer for my breakdown. It was without a doubt caused by a combination of studying, reading until the tiny hours of the morning, the stress of my job at the drugstore, the constant stress surrounding my finances, and the general tension that invades the essence of us all. Having said that, I have to this day carefully kept and protected Ransom's brief conjectures about my lack of literary merit. They are in the same stout folder, behind stiff plastic, next to more positive, more encouraging brief notes from both Marianne Moore and the dean of modern American poetry, William Carlos Williams, who said that I possessed "an understanding of the American idiom" and showed "excellent" ability at writing poetry. Let me requote, for the millionth time, Blanche DuBois from Tennessee Williams's masterful *A Streetcar Named Desire*: "I have always relied on the kindness of strangers." In my case, such kindness served as a necessary balm against the equal measures of heartlessness that could be doled out by not only strangers but by those at arm's reach.

My experience with Ransom's scorn was my introduction to dealing with the famed of the literary world. And I was ignorant when I left Butler University. I was still uneducated after hundreds of hours of instruction. But I knew at last that what they spoke was a fact: I no longer had to wear an O'Neill mask of suffering and tragedy; it had slowly but finally etched itself into the skin of my face and the flesh of my soul.

fifteen

Convalescence

The two most important female influences on my life were my mother and my Aunt Jennie Sanford. The two most influential males were of course my father and Werner Beyer. For most of my adult lives these same four people have decidedly influenced me and my writing, frequently featuring as its subject, whether implicitly or explicitly. It was not an easy matter to shrug away the shattering judgments of Marz and Ransom, but they eventually ceased to rankle under my skin. When I pick up the pen—and I still write every one of my works first with a pen on paper rather than directly typing them into a machine—I no longer hear their phrases in my ear. The words I hear, the sound advice, the right suggestions, and the encouragingly positive criticisms are in the voice of Beyer. He was not a famous personage, simply a fine human being, a more-than-adequate scholar, and a fabulous teacher, one to appreciate for life.

It is traditional, customary with Native people that a small child's education not be left in the hands of the biological parents. This is to ensure that parents neither smother the child with doting, overly permissive love and affection, nor crush him or her with neglect and derision. In that near-perfect Native system, the task of educating children falls to the mother's sister and the father's brother. These sisters and brothers are physically removed from the natal womb, but they serve as a kind of metaphysical parallel to it. They are entrusted to care for the child's development of spirit, mind, and body in such a manner that it will ensure strengths and success in adolescence and on into more mature years. Such children are destined to be a credit to the biological family and to the extended family of the clan, and will bring honor to the tribe (or band) and nation. It was in keeping with tradition that my mother's sister, Jennie Sanford, became one of my first teachers. Our neighbors, Flo and Etta, did their part as well, as did Peg Greenwood, my mother's longtime friend. My father's only half-brother, Eugene, lived in Canada, and my father didn't socialize with many other men (at least not in my presence), so there weren't many options for adult male role models in my life until I got to Butler. As much as I admired them individually, Rocco and Cigar and Joe and David were not serious candidates for that part. Werner Beyer, however, became my surrogate father and became my guide, not only academically but also in realms that lay far beyond those ivied halls in Indianapolis. He accepted this burden probably without even considering the potential problems, and certainly without any inkling that Native people observed such a custom. Beyer's own sons lived in Chicago with their mother, his first wife from whom he had been divorced for several years when I met him. We dovetailed our needs.

I actually augmented this arrangement with a number of older men during my undergraduate years. Among them was my first boss in Indianapolis, the manager of the Parkview Drive-In, where I served hamburgers and milk shakes on trays that fastened to car windows. Another was the manager of Haag's Drugstore, who was my boss for several years during my time at Butler. Both of these men were thoughtful and recognized that I was a struggling, but (mostly) conscientious student at the university. From their keen-eyed and sympathetic perspectives, it may have seemed I was a son without a concerned father, although that was not true. My father was perpetually worried that I would not make it through this rugged life, a life with fangs eager to gobble up the frail. Despite my setbacks and violations, I wasn't as effete as my father believed. The world was also a major teacher pushing me toward maturity and development, as a person and as a poet.

It seems now that my father was always bringing me home. He had fetched me back from Bayonne when I had preferred the company of autograph hounds to schoolmates and teachers, rescuing me from the potentially harsh sentence of a judge in the process. And after I was released from the mental ward in Indianapolis, he brought me home again, this time sending my sister and her husband instead of coming to do the deed himself. His home remained my home, even when I roamed far away from Watertown, until he died in 1957, when I was twenty-eight years old.

He saved my life twice.

Now, back in my father's house once more, I was afforded time to reflect and meditate. My urge to write was a molten, flowing need. I read voraciously everything my hands touched, particularly the plays of Eugene O'Neill and Shakespeare and the poems of Robinson Jeffers and Louise Bogan. I was back in a small town, a farming community, a community, a place not half as sophisticated as Indianapolis. However, I had the opportunity of exploring the land again. In high school I had spent much time horseback riding over what were called the State Street Hills, the western foothills of the Adirondacks. No longer a high school sophomore but a college graduate and a would-be Wordsworth, I wandered these hills, hiking in the spring and summer. I'm not sure what I was seeking: peace, probably; beauty, surely; and maybe to touch in to some vision, some spiritual quest. My own personal Tintern Abbey. When I wasn't working for my father in his business, I spent my free time in the hills, wandering, contemplating, breathing in the serene beauty. I could stand on a hill's summit and see the St. Lawrence River valley and imagine Akwesasne off in the very far distance. On clear days, I could make out the green and blue Adirondacks with my naked eyes and through binoculars. I roamed the flowered fields, strolled the shores of the Black River, and burned away the night composing poems. Many nights, my father would enter my bedroom and quietly turn out the lamp, knowing I had exhausted my mind and spirit. The hills and rivers helped heal my dark soul and damaged mind. My father's unwavering support completed this difficult task.

My writing continued, or words . . . rather, words and rhythms . . . continued to pour from my imagination and out through my pen. I became more confident, found new images or freshened old ones, explored new objects and ideas. I had something to write about, not merely the wanton joys of youth; in any case, youth was seeping figuratively through my fingers, getting away from me. No, I was finally growing as a writer and a man, though many have said that a poet can never fully resolve into an adult and must cling to at least some of the trappings of youth. Where else will he find the freshness to work out of and into the poems? I've been called young for my age well into my eighties, but whether that means I retained my youth or just that I remained immature is best left to others to judge. Instead of concerning myself with the opinions of learned men, I once more caught the scent of chicory on the winds, smelled the ripe wild strawberries. I observed the flight of birds, especially the red-tailed hawk, which hunted the surrounding valleys and the woods of the hills.

sixteen

Cathy B.

Amazing! I don't really know how or where we met. Perhaps at a bar or a music store? We both enjoyed a fine red wine and classical music, which was never heard in either of our homes. My father enjoyed country and her family was deep into pop songs by Frank Sinatra, Patti Page, Rosemary Clooney, among others. We must have met under strange circumstances, such as the cliché would dictate. Watertown at that time had at least two rather fancy cocktail lounges; one was located in the Hotel Woodruff on Public Square and the other up the street on the second floor of a building that had been a Chinese restaurant. I don't have a name in memory, but it was a tad fancy, filled with middle-class people, both locals and traveling salesmen, looking for a girl or a guy, depending on their tastes. The art crowd, such as it was, hung out there as well, though some frequented the classier Black River Club, which catered to the wealthy folk in town. I can't think of any place I would have met Cathy other than in a cocktail bar, but still it might very well have been the one music store we had on Arsenal Street, which sold long-playing record albums of Broadway show tunes, some of the more popular country music, and certainly classical composers such as Mozart, Bartók, Mahler, and the like.

We went always to her home off in the small country village of Dexter, New York. She lived there with both her mother and older brother. Strange, but I never met either and have really no sound idea why not; I can only guess that her mother retired early in the evening and her brother was usually out. Cathy always burned candles for light, even though electricity had made it to Dexter decades earlier. We'd pop a bottle of wine, a cheap but tasty Chianti, and spin our records. Our conversations concerned music or travel or my returning to the university for graduate school. Cathy thought it best I go to Syracuse University, but I was not quite sure, as my father had designs on me going to Columbia in New York City. That would satisfy me, but Cathy had a good job as a nurse to my father's medical doctor and her thought was that she could continue working and help me attend university closer to home. A good idea, but it didn't work.

My father soon learned of our friendship and questioned me about it. "Yes," I told him, "we have been friends this spring and summer." He was not happy to hear this and made it known. He insisted that if my shrink deemed me fit enough to return to school after my breakdown, then I *must* go to New York and enter Columbia. He would help me with paying tuition. Another good idea . . . in principle, at least.

Cathy questioned nothing but the music we listened to, the weak poetry we were scrawling onto scrap paper, and possibly if we shouldn't have been buying a better class of wine than the wicker-wrapped Chianti we quaffed. We were in full bloom, sort of in love . . . or feeling that way, moving into our sensations of early adulthood. We felt like we were on the top of the Empire State Building, or would be soon enough. Life was good, the wine tasty, the music dark and often dreary, but both lent their vibrations to us. We were not much more than kids with the cliché of life stretching out before us. We both wished to be writers, specifically poets, and knew we would have to do something about it; the cultural climate in Watertown was not sufficiently Bohemian for our growing tendencies. We had to get out of this hometown of ours, where nothing would grow and mature but the numbers on the calendar. And we who seemed to act like kids considered ourselves already on the brink of middle age . . . or at least somewhere close to it. We had to go, we had to run, or fly or simply drive out of this dead city. The route would take us through Syracuse University to Manhattan, where we would strike gold and dance to the tune of our own piper, ourselves.

What a life sat there waiting for us to pick up. Oh! School . . . no, *university*! This plot was well laid! My father had told me enough times to convince me that you don't make a million dollars from poetry . . . or anything . . . at the start, if ever. Get a degree and teach, or work in a Korean fruit stand, or write poetry eighteen hours a day, whatever . . . but do the work that you're most likely to do for your entire life. That facet was ground deep into the work ethic he passed on to me and I've never forgotten it over the course of the sixty years since I left Watertown.

New York City seemed a million miles from Syracuse, and Syracuse was equally distant from our wishes and hopes, but it was going to have to be a necessary waystation for us. If everything went as planned, we'd spend two long, possibly torturous, years there before being able to move on to New York. Other than those intended years in a holding pattern, time did not occur to us. Nor did money or where it might come from; we did not have any and my father surely would not write a check that was not addressed to Columbia University. It was decided that Cathy would come to Syracuse and work while I studied.

She would quit her nursing job in Watertown and try to find something similar in Syracuse, perhaps at the city's teaching hospital, which had only recently become affiliated with SUNY at that point.

They were great plans, worthy of mice, men, and me. We laughed and sipped more wine, turned on more magical music and allowed our crazy scheme/dream to develop. We were sitting on my father's couch plotting the route. Cathy would drive her Chevy at midnight, having explained to her boss that she had to leave town for a time . . . perhaps she'd tell him there was a sickness in her family. My task was simpler; all I needed to do was pack a bag, wait for her to pick me up, and I was free as an eagle.

Never did we guess that my father was standing at the top of the stairs, out of sight, listening in on our plans for the future . . . plans that didn't involve consulting his wishes. I imagine him with his fists rubbing together, screaming inside his head: ". . . and after all I did for this thankless kid, look how he just wants to throw it away! He has no sense, no vision! What gave him the foolish idea to run off with this idiotic woman without so much as a change of shoes or two pairs of clean underwear?"

As it happened, Cathy cut her hand rather badly at work the next day. Consequently, we had to defer our elopement for several days, which gave my father just enough time to gather his wits and destroy our plan. The first thing he did was to hurry to the doctor's office. He claimed that Cathy was a prostitute and that he needed to fire her as she was probably infected with some "social disease." Next, he drove to her mother's home in Dexter and spoke with her older brother. He also told him that she was a prostitute, and used the fact of her hanging out in the bars on Public Square in downtown Watertown as evidence. Naturally, he used these false accusations against her to explode our plan to elope. Upon arriving home from his slanderous errands, he must have reared back, smiled, and figuratively patted himself on the back for saving his stupid . . . well, not very bright, anyway . . . son from the worst tragedy man ever created: marriage.

Cathy's boss, the good doctor, called her brother, and then spoke with her, firing her over the telephone. Her brother, on learning of her alleged profession and the possibility of running away with me, caused an outcry in the household. Her mother threatened to lock her in her room. Her brother said he would never speak to her again and that he should punish her for her stupidity and foolishness, and for the shame she had brought upon her family. She should be horsewhipped and possibly placed in a jail cell until she came to her senses and had cleansed her thoughts, much less her body and soul.

We again reshuffled our elopement hour, but didn't cancel it. If anything, the way she had been treated made it clear why she couldn't stay. Two nights later, I sat on my father's couch again aggravated and stupefied, waiting for Cathy's car to motor up the driveway. A small sack of clothes lay at my feet, a few books . . . I recall volumes of Robert Frost's poetry, some plays of Eugene O'Neill . . . and a wish that this escapade was complete. I heard my father running water in the bathroom. He would turn it on, then off, then on, then off. The phone shrieked throughout the house. Before I could grab it, my father held it to his ear. I heard him put the receiver down and heard him hasten down the stairs, a rapid series of clumps, one at a time.

"Well, young idiot. Your plot has been discovered and destroyed. She left a number for you to call her when you are up to it, but I should tell you, she won't be coming for you tonight." I remember he gave a huge yawn and turned to look at my prone, puzzled figure on the couch. "Oh yes, I near forgot to tell you. She is already almost to Detroit." Having delivered his message, he went to bed at last. His work was completed.

A day or so later I did receive a telephone call from Cathy, claiming to be in Detroit. She was crying, and her words were nearly indistinguishable. "I am going to kill myself! I'm so ashamed of what your father and my brother have done to me! I am so ashamed! I don't ever want to see you again!" There was no way I could ease her pain, and my emotions were such a mix of confusion, abandonment, and relief that I didn't know what to say to her. I did know that it was the definite end of what had been a crazy plan.

Two years later I bumped into Cathy in the streets of Manhattan. She was dressed in a lovely floral knee-length dress. She was smiling and laughing and clutching the arm of a young woman . . . also very pretty. They seemed very happy, though the reasons for their happiness were ones I could only surmise. It was not an age, even in Manhattan, during which you would ask a person such a thing or expect a truthful answer in response. Whatever the reason, her smile upon our parting marked the end of my first close call with matrimony.

seventeen

St. Lawrence

Roy Marz made two mistakes. First, he attempted to deny that I had any talent as a poet, to dampen my lyrical urges. The second mistake Marz made was to introduce me to the poetry of both William Carlos Williams and Robinson Jeffers, especially the latter's rock-hard poems. Jeffers became my staff of inspiration. One poem alone—"Hurt Hawks"—brought me into the surrealism of conscious dreaming:

> The broken pillar of the wing jags from the clotted shoulder,
> The wing trails like a banner in defeat,

That had been me. I was the hawk.

> He wandered over the foreland hill and returned in the evening, asking
> for
> death,
> Not like a beggar, still eyed with the old
> Implacable arrogance. I gave him the lead gift in the twilight. What fell
> was relaxed,
> Owl-downy, soft feminine feathers; but what
> Soared: the fierce rush: the night-herons by the river cried fear at its
> rising
> Before it was quite unsheathed from reality.

I knew from Iroquois lore, tradition, that the hawk was the messenger of the people to the spirit world. The poet was also a messenger. I became the hawk, the poet, and the messenger, as I would later write in a poem called simply "The Hawk":

I rise morning after morning
And walk through the wet meadows
Though I never frighten off the hawk
With a gun or with a cry,
But I have sometimes held
It bread an bits of meat
To coax it from the sky.

His talons drip with honey,
His beak is full of gentian leaves
And blossoms, and his eye
Shines with a strange kindness
As his feathers dust the sky.

What drives the babe to suck
And kneads the blood with passion;
What tickles idiots
And has them laugh
Drives my hand to clutch
His feathers and wear
Them in an ancient fashion.

Many years later, I dined at the home of the avant-garde poet-editor Kirby Congdon. With a golden goblet of wine in his right hand, he exclaimed that when he first read "The Hawk" he learned to hate me. Smiling, of course, he added that the hatred was because I had written a marvelous poem and it had been published in my first book, *Dead Letters Sent*, whereas he had not as yet published a book. I was several years younger than him. Kirby's remark was meant to be a compliment, though he was known for his crankiness. He also informed me that "The Hawk" was the first contemporary Native American poem he'd ever read.

That was a delightful evening—above and beyond his kind words. At his table that night, assisting him in all his host's duties was his companion, Ralph Simmons. Kirby had assembled a charming guest list. Robert Peters was visiting New York City, offering a reading of his poems at the nearby Poetry Society of America, I believe. It was our first introduction. Also at the table sat two most extraordinary women: the late Barbara Holland, and the unique Helen Adam—both poets of tremendous talents. Years later, I became closely acquainted with both these women. In fact, Contact/II, the press and journal I oversaw for many years, brought out a posthumous collection of Barbara Holland's. Helen and

I dined many times. I was fascinated by her and her ballads, especially the sea shanties she composed so bizarrely and with such deftness.

My response to Kirby's exclamation about my poem was that it never would have been conceived, much less written down, had Robinson Jeffers not awakened the inclination in me to probe not only the flight of hawks and their spirit, but also the nature of death. The poem was written thinking back to "Hurt Hawks," and simultaneously my school days at Butler and my stupid attempt at suicide while there. Jeffers opened my eyes and spirit to image and symbol. At last I had begun to understand the incomprehensible, the magic of poems, the undiscovered, dreams, and the memories that turn into dreams as dream coats the hurt and pain in many colors. Such a hurt is so deep, so painful, that memory must bury it or we cannot survive. Bury the seed or the bulb of the wild plant so that eventually, come spring, it will rise out of the earth and blossom. My poem "The Hawk" was the result of burying my hurt, my shattered illusion, my fragmented dream, the broken glass in the kaleidoscope of youth, in the most tender flesh and sinew. Instead of killing the hawk, Marz had presented me with a challenge. I would prove him wrong . . . and Ransom at the same time.

It is so easy to slip into maudlin sentimentality when reviving, revising, the early cracked years of one's youth, to remember too much thunder, too many roses, too much blood and hellish screams. As one tries to get outside the reverie, the brain's stockpile of vivid remembrances, scenes, and actions never, never lost, perhaps multiplied or made saccharine by time. I might say Robinson Jeffers saved my life while Gerard Manley Hopkins and A. E. Housman saved my soul. Wordsworth did nothing for me, other than causing me to compose the worst poems I've ever written . . . it's not that he is a bad poet, but I was a bad student to his poetry.

I dallied with Robert Frost and T. S. Eliot, but Frost's rhymes stuck in my craw and continued to remind me of Ransom's prediction. Eliot, who wrestled with his own spirit, his faith, continued to have some effect on me, but I abandoned his lessons because his faith led him in a different direction from the one in which I insisted on traveling. He had turned to Europe and Judeo-Christian belief, and I honestly did not wish to go that road. Jeffers (and the other writers who would follow him in influencing me) and my muse—for lack of a better term—demanded I stay in this ancient world that some call America, here "on the turtle's back." As Eliot immersed himself in Christianity and literary criticism and French symbolism, I moved forward into the newness of the old to revive the ancient strengths of this land, this earth, yet, even these waters and this sky. The winds that tapped my pen were from the four corners, the four directions of the ruins of a tribal society Eliot . . . like so many others . . . had ignored. His sails were blown by ocean winds; mine came down off the mountains. Perhaps I clung tighter to Frost than I thought all these years. I unmistakably clung to Edwin Arlington Robinson, though, and to a poet from Canada, a Mohawk woman not a widely recognized as those gentlemen, but a poet who is respected and remains in print even though she died in semi-obscurity in Vancouver, British Columbia, in 1913. E. Pauline Johnson—grandmother to Native American poets, a Mohawk who did not renounce the Indian in herself—survived, as did Native songs and stories through her work. She had no fear and possessed much talent. She has remained a flag breathing in the same air as the reputable and resilient hawk, and her work survives in a world where poetry is neither read nor respected. Poetry is a career that receives little applause from any nation or community because society believes it can exist and maintain life without the heartbeat, the indomitable spirit, of poetry. Fortunately, Johnson's literary grandchildren have continued to pay the respect of admiration, and her poems—though often didactic and sometimes a touch too purple—have remained indelibly stamped in printer's ink, and they stand on the bookshelf with others of her kind and breed.

We may be a vanishing crop. Our harvest doesn't fare well in the market today. Our society thinks—and I stress, *thinks*—it can do without us, although that is far from the truth. The very soul of humankind is the spirit of poetry. Without it I should have remained in the shadowy ward in the Indianapolis hospital with the black youth combing my hair over and over again, or my "pillars of the wing" would still "jag from the clotted shoulder." Poetry may have damned me, but it has also proven to be my sustenance. It was my corn, the venison of my life, and I believe it is the nutrition of all human life, its spirit. Without it we are doomed to petrify: ceremony will cease; a space venture to Mars will never happen; gardens will wither; children will be born old; and meadowlarks will no longer sing.

In the fall of 1956, I wisely registered at St. Lawrence University, specifically, at its extension campus in Watertown. I'm occasionally amazed at how very bright I can be; I can even have enough intelligence to do the right thing, or make the correct or important choice . . . albeit perhaps with a misstep or two (or ten) along the way. I signed up for a survey of English literature with a professor, Douglas Angus, who I later learned was not only Canadian-born but, like Roy Marz, a published author . . . though Angus's medium of choice was fiction rather than poetry. I felt safe under his care. Nevertheless, I made sure that he could not embarrass or hurt me by rejecting my poetic output, because I wouldn't admit to him that I was composing poems.

Douglas Angus was a godsend, another man who saved my life, albeit more figuratively than some others. He encouraged me away from Whitman and Eliot, and decidedly away from Wordsworth. He gently pushed me closer to Keats, Jeffers, Williams, Hopkins, Faulkner, and Bogan. Robinson likewise became important to me at this time, while Dylan Thomas . . . so easy to imitate poorly and so difficult to emulate well . . . began to fall away from my view as though a wiper's blade had swept him off my glass. He was not to be forgotten entirely, but no longer would serve me as an influence. Frost also was relegated to textbooks; his photo no longer was tacked to my studio wall so that it faced out, or down, onto where my pencils and typewriter lay. Faulkner took his place and has remained a fixture there since.

Angus held sway over my poetic imagination more strongly than anyone until I entered New York University and began studying with Louise Bogan. Later Willard Motley, and later yet, Leslie Marmon Silko and Simon J. Ortiz, would fill these central roles in my creative thought processes, but then, in 1956, I was wrapped up in the congenial and yet explosive tutelage of Douglas Angus. Until his death in 2002, I enjoyed visiting him in his Canton home, and I used his fine anthology, *The Best Short Stories of the Modern Age*, as an instructor throughout my career. Like many comparable anthologies, his includes the remarkable Faulkner story "A Rose for Emily." He had once remarked that Faulkner was a weak writer and not worthy of a read, let alone study. I was required to write a term paper for one of his courses and had read *As I Lay Dying*, which moved me deeply. Consequently, I chose to write on Faulkner, titling my paper something like "The Symbol as Moral." Angus refused to give me permission, but when I protested, he finally relented and honored my request. I believe I received an A- on the paper, but more important to me than the grade was what he wrote on the title page: "My apology. You have proven Faulkner worthy." I have often wondered if my paper had anything to do with "A Rose for Emily" being selected for his very well-regarded anthology, which is still in print decades after its initial appearance.

I cannot recall exactly which works of Shelley he directed us to read. I know we read Frost's "The Silken Tent," which did not much attract me, and his fabulous "The Witch of Coos," which has remained a lifelong favorite, even as other Frost has waned in my esteem. In any case, Angus asked us to write a brief paper on a Shelley poem. At the end of the class period and on the way to the door, he stopped me while I was getting into my coat. It was winter then and cold, snow flurried outside; it was more a Frost night than a Shelley one. "And you, young man," he said, "you can't hide from me under that bulky coat. You, young man, are a poet. And therefore I want you to compose your essay on Shelley in verse!" He started to walk off as if I had been dismissed, a curious manner of expression he retained throughout his life.

It was as though Zeus himself had struck me with an enormous charge of lightning. I gasped, shuddered, and began shaking. The cold night air whipped at my chin. Falling in behind him, the general, I tugged at his overcoat sleeve and stuttered that I was not a poet, that I never wrote poems. Like a train slamming into a stone wall, he abruptly stopped, oblivious to the snowflakes falling around his ears and upraised coat collar: "You can't hide it, son. I know you write poems. Nearly everything you write is poetical, lyrical. I want you to compose the essay on Shelley in verse. And furthermore, I want you to bring me your poems to read." He turned, left me in the flurries of snow, flakes sticking to my eyelashes, to my warm lips, and figuratively to my leaping heart, to my joy. My secret been discovered . . . and not deemed unworthy.

Despite that, I must admit that the essay I wrote on Shelley was stupid, idiotic garbage. Angus expected that. He knew that what he asked of me would likely not work, but was worth trying and failing at. I also brought him the poems he requested, poems like "The Hawk," "The Hopeless Kill," "Four: In the Chinese Manner," and "Noon." It seems to me now that he made no technical, written comments on the separate pages I gave to him, but he did remain after class one night and discussed the work with me in person. Unlike Marz, he showed approval for my young raw talent. I explained Marz and Ransom's critical position; I spoke of Beyer's appreciation. Angus just nodded his lion-like head. Douglas Angus was a very tall, thin man. I always thought he would have made a sensational Scarecrow in the *Wizard of Oz* except that his stance was stiff, unbending, more like the Tin Man in the throes of rust. Just his stance, though, not his outlook on life. He was a university professor to the hilt, the perfect stereotype. He also was a compassionate man with a rich sensibility and a heart that could reveal its warmth even in a snowstorm. He told me, simply and directly, "You must continue to write poems. You are very good; have much to learn, much to live and experience; much to read, hopefully to show you the way. But you have a god-given talent. Perhaps since that other teacher examined your poems, you have developed a sensibility. Now go home and write more."

eighteen

Amid the Bookshelves

Angus's comments gave me a renewed sense of discipline, responsibility, motivation, and drive, but I also knew that the home to which I would return and write would not be in Watertown. In the fall of 1957, I once again left the North Country with my father's blessing . . . apparently, I had still not exhausted his patience. I rode the Greyhound to New York, determined to enter Columbia University that following spring. Upon arriving, I took Columbia's entrance exams, which I passed, though hardly in glowing neon. The examinations were tough, and the math questions most probably lowered my overall grade. Still, I was invited to enroll at Columbia in June of 1958, which meant I needed to find a rented room and a job for the intervening months. The room I found was in West Greenwich Village at 66 Morton Street, a street arched over with trees. The house was only a block away from the painting studio of the poet e. e. cummings. I stood for hours, in snow and rain, watching for the great man to exit. I managed to see his shadow once or twice. I also was fortunate to see Frank Lloyd Wright during the building of his Guggenheim Museum, a masterpiece of architecture, and I managed a glimpse of Carl Sandburg strolling around the fountain in Washington Square, hugging his guitar. So close was I to creativity and fame.

The job I found was as a dollar-an-hour clerk in the Marboro bookstore on East Fifty-Ninth Street, not far from the Hotel Pierre and from F.A.O. Schwartz, neither of which could I ever dream of entering. I worked diligently at the "remainder book shop," and I loved my labors. My boss was generous in teaching me the ins and outs of the retail book business, and in no less than three months I found myself managing the store. Needless to say, I did not enter Columbia that following June. The Marboro was attuned to the artistic pulse of the city, and many celebrities shopped with us. Not far off were Carnegie Hall and the Art Students League. We were a few steps from the "Great White Way" of the legitimate theater. The palatial movie houses lit up Broadway a half-dozen blocks from the store, and so on. A favorite customer was the handsome

Jeff Chandler, a good Jewish actor who played many Indian roles, as was common in those days. I remember Cochise as being one. Clerking for me was the young and impressionable college-aged daughter of Dr. Robert E. Rothenberg, who was famed for authoring the very popular book *Understanding Surgery*. She was entranced by Chandler. She was five-and-a-half feet tall at most, while he was broad-shouldered and stood well over six feet. The first time he entered the shop while she was there, she looked up into his face and fainted upon recognizing him.

It was at the Fifty-Ninth Street Marboro location that I hired the poet Asa Benveniste, of *Zero* magazine renown. Not only was he well published and respected, but he had composed an introduction for the novel *Brothers and Sisters*, by Ivy Compton-Burnett, who at that time was a favorite writer of mine. I was thrilled to have Asa work for me, even if it was only for a few months before he moved to England. He was generous, but honest in his appraisal of my own poetry, and especially of the poems that later went into *Dead Letters Sent*.

We did not have these critical sessions while at work, though. Asa critiqued my poems at the old White Horse Bar in Greenwich Village, made famous first by Dylan Thomas and later by Brendan Behan, the playwright. Any night of the week after closing time you were allowed to drink beer in a small, crowded backroom and listen to the Clancy Brothers sing out their drunken Irish hearts till dawn. I became friendly with Tom Clancy (the singer, not the writer), and years later we were neighbors in Brooklyn Heights. They were marvelous singers and the women thronged to them. The White Horse was a bastion of fun, hilarity, and cheap beer. The melee of poets and artists was staggering. But shortly thereafter the bar lost its bohemian appeal; the Clancy brothers went off to fame, and the artsy crowd moved to the Cedar Bar on University Place. The Cedar was less known for poets, though it became recognized as a hangout for such painters as Larry Rivers and Jackson Pollock. Frank O'Hara could still be found there from time to time.

My service as manager of the Fifty-Ninth Street Marboro was short-lived. My immediate supervisor, John Zito, informed me late one Friday of my promotion to manager of the Fifty-Seventh Street Marboro, a change that was to take effect the following Monday. This shop, situated between Sixth Avenue and Seventh Avenue, was only a few doors from the Russian Tea Room and Carnegie Hall. Here the buds of my life began to open petal by petal, but I also sprouted thorn after thorn. I spent six years in that shop bending to the rich and famous and learning the numbers and the corresponding titles in Random House's Modern Library catalogue. I swept and mopped floors, ordered books, hired and fired employees, appeased irate customers, apprehended shoplifters, soothed the ruffled feathers of the famous, paid off firemen with stuffed envelopes in the back bathroom, shelved books, dressed the front window, went to night court to prosecute thieves, and built up the store's inventory to include an excellent collection of art books, poetry, classics literature, modern fiction, cookbooks, and gardening manuals for city dwellers and suburbanites alike.

I began dealing with salespeople directly from the publishers. I remember ordering twelve copies of Nabokov's newly published and quickly banned *Lolita*, for which I definitely had customers. Fred Weitzman, the company's president and my boss, received the shipment in his downtown office. Fearing a government lawsuit, he returned the books to the original publisher, Olympia Press. I'd had the same problem with Henry Miller's *Tropic of Cancer* and D. H. Lawrence's *Lady Chatterley's Lover*, both of which had also been banned in the United States. I was not so much interested in challenging the morality of the day, but rather in making sales and upping my daily receipts. Remember, even though Joyce's *Ulysses* had not been banned, it was still kept in the library backroom in those days because of Leopold Bloom's sexual and defecatory urges. Likewise, Edmund Wilson's *Memoirs of Hecate County* was both a best-seller and banned by the Supreme Court until 1959. What people wanted and what we were allowed or encouraged to sell them did not match up very well. Mr. Weitzman was a good man and held my respect. A moral, law-abiding citizen, he also was decidedly a businessman. At his insistence, I was soon out of the "pornography" business.

The Fifty-Seventh Street Marboro afforded me a pretty exciting life, but not because I grew rich on the salary. I was making $75 a week, a marginal improvement from the $1 an hour I was making as a clerk. No, the excitement came from the location in the epicenter of Manhattan's arts culture and from the quality and diversity of my clerking staff and the store's many habitual customers, my clientele. Next door, but actually in the same building, was a movie house that screened films from France and other European countries as well as ones imported from Japan. I attended often, as the pictures were usually better than good, occasionally excellent . . . and *always* better than the movie house further along Broadway in Times Square. These movies were very popular with transplanted Europeans and assorted bohemian folk who thought to tip ushers.

Among the clerks who worked for me were actors (Nick Smith and Michael Badge), painters (George Ortman, then married to the actress Carol Bavossa; and Charles Dudley, who gave me the cover drawing for my book *And Grieve, Lesbia*), photographers, and a film director (Gregory Markopoulos). Few writers worked at the store, and none whom I remember by name. Why so few writers sought employment in a bookstore, what would seem a likely place in which to find them, I have no idea. Perhaps they worked as waiters or in the libraries instead, preferring not to sell books other than their own.

I still have on the bookshelf near my writing desk a collection of short stories published first in the *New Yorker* magazine. The book was presented to me in 1960 as a Christmas gift by my staff. I can read the inscribed signatures: "Nick, Ed, George, Michael, Charles Dudley." I recall that Ed was a writer, but I don't think he ever found any fame at it. All of these men were heavy readers, and I allowed them to borrow books from the stock. They couldn't afford to buy many on their meager salary of a dollar an hour, especially since most of these young men worked only part-time. They were all good men, and I remember them with fondness and gratitude for giving their all, excelling at what might have seemed a demeaning job. I remember saying one morning to Nick, "How is it that I never have to tell you to sweep the floor?" It was as if I had struck him on the cheek. He reared back, studied a moment, smiled, and answered, "I couldn't stand being told to sweep the floor. I'd quit. Thank God, you never commanded me to."

Not many of those men ended up gaining a great reputation in his chosen artistic field. Nick Smith also acquired some off-Broadway roles in various plays. One production I remember was John Heffernan's staging of Shaw's *Androcles and the Lion*. I recall that Nick carried a spear, though whether he spoke or not escapes me. Mike Hadge appeared in numerous films and TV shows, most famously on *Dark Shadows* in the late sixties. Charley Dudley became night manager of a Greenwich Village bookstore on Eighth Street.

There were a couple of exceptions, though. A year or so after leaving the shop, George Ortman showed his work at a prestigious gallery, The Stable, to huge crowds . . . and sold many of his paintings for considerable prices. George was indeed a most creative artist, and his creativity deserves the attention. A short, pale-faced man whose clothes were always splattered with the colors of his current work, he was a walking palette. There was always, every morning, a sweat-ring around the collar of his rumpled and grayed white shirt. Marboro had a dress code, and several times I had to send him home for a tie. A nice fellow, George, but he did not have much interest in selling books, at least not in the way our mutual employer wanted him to.

The death in autumn of 1992 of another of my clerks, Gregory Markopoulos, came as a surprise. His obituary appeared in the *New York Times* alongside that of my friend, the most gifted black, feminist, lesbian poet—as she was wont to say of herself—Audre Lorde. Audre's death seemed imminent from almost the first evening we met, but still is something with which I have not been able to truly reconcile myself. I found Gregory to be somewhat unkempt and argumentative, and he carried with him an odor of grease and garlic. He was a full-blooded Greek. By that I don't mean to imply that all Greeks smell—they don't—but Gregory certainly did. The skin of his cheek and brow nearly always had a shine. His clothes were appropriate for his work, but not necessarily fashionable. Like Ortman, his white shirts were usually dingy. His fellow staff members did not consider him particularly bright . . . we all thought he lived in a fantasy world, and those early years of his directorial career, marked as they were with unsuccessful and unfinished projects, suggested little more than failure to us. He was working on a film that would eventually become *Twice a Man*. He filmed his story on the Staten Island ferry, among other places. Money was impossible for him to raise after he'd struggled to complete a feature film called *Serenity* that he'd expensively shot back in Greece. He had no money of his own, only a simple job at Marboro. He needed a musical score for the sound track and could not afford to hire an orchestra or obtain permission from a record company. I rented him my radio for five dollars a week, so he could tape classical music. As soon as his film was completed, he disappeared from the store and my memory. I never saw him again, though his reputation as an avant-garde director certainly grew afterward.

nineteen

My Beautiful Rose

While managing the Marboro, I met the only other woman besides Cathy that I ever wanted to marry . . . and I also met my lifelong best friend. Rose was a Puerto Rican woman who worked in Manhattan but lived with her family in the South Bronx. She was very interested in movies and the theater, and we nearly always attended one or the other when we dated. A charming, bright, clever, gorgeous woman. She remains in my dreams and my guilt overwhelms me in my sleep. We should have married. My life would have been different.

During the summer of 1960, I was managing the Marboro branch on West Fifty-Seventh Street. One day, I received a phone call from the company's home office. It was a high female voice, a woman who proved most discerning in her cinematic and dramatic tastes (as I quickly found out, having diverted the conversation from the book business about which she had called). She asked if I might possibly get her a free seat at such-and-such showing of such-and-such movie at the Film House movie theater. I said that I thought I could and would see about taking care of it, provided that I could use my extensive experience from years before to usher her to her seat. She agreed to my terms and told me that her name was Rose. She arrived minutes before six o'clock for a six-fifteen showing. I was struck hard. She was beautiful. Rose was more than beautiful . . . my height or a tad smaller, slender almost to the point of being thin, she held a fine, graceful carriage. Her skin was a natural cinnamon complexion; her speech held a trace of a Spanish accent and also a touch of the Bronx. I was totally bowled over, entranced. I saw her to her seat and whispered, "Might we have a drink after your film?" She gorgeously smiled and replied, "Yes." And she did so with no hesitation, as I happily noted. Rose had an unforgettable smile. Her lips spread from side to side, allowing a look at her white teeth, which lit up the night. With her single word began a long romance!

We met after the showing. We went to the Carnegie Grill, which at that time was a German restaurant that served sauerbraten and frothy dark beer. We chatted over two or three steins and ended by making a date for the following week, agreeing to meet again at the Film House to see whatever new film would have opened by then. Naturally, I also planned to take her back to the same restaurant for frothy beers and conversation, since it had worked so well the first time. My heart beat ten miles a minute. This gorgeous woman was actually my date . . . *my date*. No one else's . . . even if it was initially based upon a free ticket instead of my personal charms.

We met fairly regularly either at the movie house or the theater. Rose would have liked to have been an actor and was actually studying drama at the time. Occasionally, we might go out to an inexpensive club . . . sometimes a jazz club. We dated frequently, and she usually would allow me at the end of the evening to accompany her back home to Jackson Avenue in the South Bronx. This area was not safe for anyone at that time, let alone a short pale-skinned fellow obviously far from his usual stomping grounds in Manhattan. I would always walk her to her building from the subway, and then Rose's young brother always walked with me back to the subway. If the streets were particularly rowdy, he would even ride the train until it curved back into upper Manhattan, making sure that no one gave me trouble on the train. Then he crossed platforms and rode north to home. It was a challenge, but Rose was obviously worth the thrills of danger.

Rose told me that when I wasn't with her, she was occasionally stopped by the cops while returning home late and questioned about whether she was out hooking. She always gave a giggle, told them who her father was . . . a well-known taxi driver in the South Bronx . . . and the police who recognized his name took her home and made sure she was safe. Rose laughed at these adventures. She knew who she was, and carried herself within a suave air.

Finally, the day came when she asked to see where I lived and whether she could pay a visit. I was terrified, and yet a tiny thrill ran through my body. I responded with smiles; even my blue eyes smiled grandly. Rose wished to see my nest and I was excited to show it to her, thrilled that she would wish to see my pad. But . . . and this was a huge but . . . I was by that time living on the Lower East Side on Norfolk Street, a predominantly Jewish neighborhood with a smattering of Hispanics and African Americans thrown in. Next door was a winery that made Manischewitz, an old traditional Jewish wine drunk mostly on holidays. The smell was outrageously strong and penetrated every corner of the street, the rooms in which you lived, and the very clothes you wore to work.

Neither the neighborhood's ethnic makeup nor its boozy fragrance presented a problem, but my neighbor Sarah might, and my occasional roommate JP might be distracted or upset by me bringing a woman home, much less one as beautiful as Rose. Despite some reservations, I decided that this was something I'd been wanting for a while and brought her home with me. Sarah and JP were two of the most important people in my city life at that time. I wondered how they would react to this young woman who might be perceived by them as being out to change their lives, at least inasmuch as their friendship with me was a part thereof.

As it happened, Sarah was the first of the two to meet Rose. She was an elderly Russian Jewess who had worked ninety percent of her long life in a sweat-box factory making children's clothing. She could barely speak English and could not write or read it. I dialed phone calls for her, read letters to her, and wrote out laundry and grocery lists for her so that she could get her chores done with relative ease. She was my newfound grandmother, but for one niggling truth: I was not, am not Jewish. But I could never convince her of this, no matter how much I protested. Whether it was about my big nose, my affected Brooklyn-like accent (about the origins of which I fear I rarely, if ever, told the truth), or some other trait that convinced her of my heritage, her reply was always . . . "Ya doant gotta be 'shemmed." Sarah actually was an old darling. She would share a banana with me when she thought I looked hungry, or she would take me to Jewish-owned markets and bargain for me . . . a broom, a plant, a handful of tomatoes at the Essex Street Market, which stood directly behind the tenement house in which I lived with JP. Sarah did not like JP very much, but she also did not fear he would interrupt our friendship like Rose (or any other girl) might. Little did she know.

JP was ensconced in his room when I brought Rose home. They said few words; in fact, he was grumpy, close to rude, and only stayed a minute before he took off. Sarah knocked, opened the door before I could do so, and entered my tenement kitchen, which was really a bath as well, complete with a bathtub filled with dirty clothes (though hidden with a thick metal cover). I introduced Sarah to Rose. Sarah gave a tiny smile, a smile that suggested she knew this young woman was up to no good, that she had designs on me. Sarah grabbed for her left hand. Pawed where a round gold ring might be found or and smirked rather pointedly. This was not the Sarah I knew and loved in a curiously grandmotherly fashion. Then she pranced out of the kitchen, leaving my door wide open. She stopped at her own door, looked back to mine, and slammed her door shut the second she was through it. Rose stayed only long enough to warn me that she had a strong feeling that JP was trouble, and that I should let him wander away and out of my life. I protested, knowing that this was not going to happen. "OK, but he *is* bad," she repeated firmly, before walking around the corner and then going north on the subway back to the Bronx. It was not the reception I had hoped for, to be sure.

For once, Rose was wrong. He was not bad, not dangerous. Headstrong, to be sure, and rather cantankerous. A lot like me in both of those regards, actually. He had been born on the island of Vieques, off the east coast of Puerto Rico, and had come to New York and the Lower East Side as a young lad. He always wanted out of the three-room apartment in which he lived with six of his relatives. He wanted out, and even before he graduated from high school he had joined the navy, because that was a way out. Yet when his tour expired he was right back on East Thirteenth Street with not much to do but hang out . . . and hanging out meant trouble. He wobbled around the city below Fourteenth Street. He roamed those areas with his cousin Plato, who did do some lawless things. But JP continued looking for a path out and he began to understand how he could do it legally. We met on an early autumnal night on Seventh Avenue in the West Village and quickly became friends. We stayed close friends for many years, in fact. We had much in common. Both of us had struggled with the lives our fathers had envisioned for us. He had older brothers. I had older sisters. I was lonely for friends. I was lonely for a brother. JP and I were crazy in love with life, with Hollywood and celebrities, with good food and decent wine, with Marilyn Monroe and Bette Davis, with the arts, writing, drawing, poems, and literature. I wrote two small booklets of poems for him. There were times when we were happy; there were times when we fought like wild cats. We were looking for life, we searched alleyways in the city, many cities, the countries of the world where we would arrive in anticipation; we wanted to go places, be there, be *somebodies*. We shared several rooms and apartments. We argued greatly, heatedly. Sometimes we were kicked out of rooms, such as on Fourteenth Street or in Little Italy, but we remained friends. Eventually, though, we split: he went off to Chicago, then on to California. I went to Mexico, to Puerto Rico, and on to the Virgin Islands. We remained friends but fought like wild tigers on the few occasions on which we met in person.

As Rose had been telling me her bad opinion of JP, Sarah had been standing next to her door listening to what words she could make out coming from my kitchen. When she at last heard the front door to my building close, she pranced back across the hallway and pounded on my door.

"You can't marry her!"

When I inquired as to why not, Sarah first blew up with a loud "Ach!" and then calmed down somewhat, speaking as gently as a worried grandmother would to a foolish grandson: "She ain't Jewish!" I replied, "I'm not Jewish either, Sarah," which only earned me a shake of the head and her stock phrase: "Ya doant gotta be 'shemmed." That was not the end of Sarah's interference in my life, though, or of her belief that I was Jewish but terribly ashamed of it. She knew real self-loathing Jews who were ashamed of their heritage, but that was not my situation.

Though JP was there in the apartment much of the time, sleeping over, tending the cat when I was away giving readings or back home in the North Country visiting family, Sarah never once questioned this bond. Obviously, she assumed he was safe, just another boy in need of some advice. As far as I could tell, she knew he wasn't Jewish, but she still seemed inclined to like him. Then one day the telephone rang. It was my mother, who at that time was still living in Bayonne. She was calling to say she that she was coming to visit soon. I was glad to hear this news, and I happened to mention my mother's visit to Sarah. She was never happier and even asked if she could serve a lunch at her kitchen table for her. I did not particularly enjoy cooking for my mother, so I gladly accepted her invitation across the hallway. A week or so later when my mother arrived, she relieved herself of her spring coat and then we walked together to Sarah's door. I knocked, and Sarah opened her door just long enough for my mother to enter and then to disappear. I did not see her for several hours. She finally returned and stayed for a few hours as we caught up on family matters.

When Sarah, again listening through her door, heard our good-byes and the sound of my door closing, she clambered across the hall and knocked loudly. I opened, and she flooded past me into the kitchen with a spryness that was unusual for her advanced age. "Kenyon" (because of her poor hearing and poor English, she always called me Kenyon or Morris, rather than Kenny or Maurice), she said, "That is *not* your mother." I was totally astonished, thunderstruck.

"Not my mother?"

"No. That woman is not your mother. She's not Jewish."

"Sarah, she *is* my mother and I am *not* Jewish."

"How many times I tell you? Ya doant gotta be 'shemmed."

After this incident Sarah stayed away for days. I'd bump into her in the hallway or the market, or walking in the street. She would always offer a smile, but she never gave up on her insistence that I had Jewish bloodlines. I had tribal connections, all right, but not the ones she thought I did.

When JP left for Chicago, it made it easier for me to spend time with Rose without worrying about his opinion of her or vice versa. Our relationship got tighter and tighter. I visited her parents in the Bronx; they were lovely people, attempting to be more American in all ways except the foods they consumed. Nothing took the place of their delicious rice and beans. I started seriously thinking of marriage around that time, but I never gave voice to those thoughts . . . much to my regret. Rose and I had a mutual friend named Virginia. Actually, Rose and Virginia were much closer that Virginia and I were. They shared more gossipy talks and enjoyed looking at and, on the rare occasions that tight finances allowed, indulging in female fashions. One early evening after I arrived home from work, Virginia phoned to say she had something quite important to reveal to me. It seems that Rose had confided in her that if I did not propose marriage in the coming two weeks, then Rose would never consider me as a prospective spouse again. After all, she needed to make choices for the benefit of her own future, and she could not, would not continue to wait in the void for me. Another man had entered her life, and so she had options if she wanted them.

I did not take the threat seriously. At the end of the two-week period, Rose announced that she was going to marry a young man who was willing to move with both her and her parents to New Jersey, where they would buy a house. Rose, my beautiful Rose, wanted out of the South Bronx badly, but it was rare that she voiced it. But why New Jersey? Why there? There was as much, if not more, discrimination for her to face in Jersey City as there was remaining in Manhattan or in the Bronx. I was certainly knocked for a loop. It took quite a while to recover from my reeling head. She followed through on her intentions and did marry the young man and move across the Hudson. Two years later, her still-young husband was in a car crash; he later died from the injuries he sustained in the accident.

I saw Rose only once more, on a subway in Manhattan a few years later. I took a seat beside her and she spoke of her husband's death. I made an attempt to console her, but I turned out to be as bad at expressing condolence to her as I had been at telling her the extent of my feelings. I stumbled off the train at my stop and never saw her again. She remains in my thoughts continuously, next to JP and my darling Sarah, who went to her grave still believing I was hiding my Jewishness. I need to say here and now I love(d) all three of them deeply.

twenty

Motley and Bogan

Women—oh, yes, yes, yes! Several, certainly . . . countable on at least my ten fingers . . . with whom I have fallen in love, even if not all of them took hold of my heart the way Cathy and Rose had. There was Connie, the piano player, with whom I cuddled when she wasn't demanding something or attempting to cut her wrists if I did not comply with her wishes. She wore mink and was a concert pianist. There was Virginia, who went to my high school but lived in the county orphanage. Her deep need to be wanted somehow drew me toward her for a while . . . until it didn't. There was a tall blonde, Caroline, whose mother suggested that I give her flowers or chocolates instead of the silver bracelet that I eventually threw into the dark waters of the Black River. I took her horseback riding, but she was too tall and lanky for me. And Ada in the West Village, who screamed when we had sex (who knew?). And I must not forget Jeanie, a beatnik who was into jazz like I was. One night, she invited me to a jazz party at her East Village apartment. Lots of guys and lots of gals. The gals were in the kitchen making a huge pot of coffee (at least I naïvely thought that's what it was) and in the living room, unfurnished in typical beatnik style, there were guys playing John Coltrane records and being "real cool," as Gwendolyn Brooks said (though not with them in mind). The women brought bowls of "coffee" into the living room. The next morning I woke up in a hill of naked bodies. It started to dawn on me that it wasn't bad coffee I had been served. I tried to pull my legs out from the pile of bodies. I never saw Jeanie again, and I walked home in the rain. Mary and I had some fun, but she turned into more of a good sister in the end, as was the case with a number of other women on a list that somewhere along the line ceased to grow except for occasional and largely unspoken inclinations at a distance.

British-born Wanda McCaddon I love dearly and in a much less fleeting way, as I suppose is evident from the fifty-plus years we have been friends. Her magic is fetching. I met her in New York and drove all the way across the country to San Francisco before traveling through Mexico together in 1962. Our journals of that time differ so greatly, our recollections . . . well, it would be difficult to figure out from reading them how we could have experienced the same trip together in the same vehicle, which we most certainly did. On our return from Mexico—which we both adored—she went out west and entered the University of California at Berkeley, where she became an E. M. Forster scholar. She later taught at UC San Diego, where she got involved with a campus theater group. She was successful at this and enjoyed performing so much that she asked to be released from her university contract and went back north again to Berkeley, which she has used as her base for a decades-long successful acting career. Her special magic has been the basis of numerous poems of mine, published, unpublished, and even in some cases unwritten. Back in the 1980s, Wanda had a part in what may possibly be the worst movie ever made in Hollywood, *Howard the Duck*. When I ribbed her, demanding that she refund me for the cost of my ticket, she said, "Joke all you want. I made money and I had a star over my dressing-room door!" Wanda has been very busy on stage, has been in a handful of films, and has gotten tons of work in TV commercials and reading books on tape. She remains a loyal friend and confidant along with her husband, Julian Block, a painter and raconteur, famed for his illustrations of Lincoln and the Civil War.

I fell in and out of love almost overnight and was convinced that I had been burned to the core by these infatuations, my life disrupted, my dreams infested, my spirit, my very soul crushed. I wrote hundreds of poems, putting Douglas Angus's advice into practice as I purged myself of these wounds. I did publish some poems in various reviews (some of which are now rather embarrassing) and in such newspapers as the *Oregonian* and the *Denver Post*. Both papers paid me one dollar for my work. My poetic forms became more contoured, projective, and imagistic, with a center pole called an object. I wrote mainly of thwarted love and sizzling passion, and penned sentimental lyrics about apple boughs and lilac scents . . . drivel. How many blossoms does the peach tree need? In real life, the number is limitless, but in poetry it is quite finite, and I took far more than my fair share in those days. I believed in my craft and talent, even if few others else did. Pain, frustrated hormones, and raw experience devised these weak and juvenile works. My poems were not taken seriously. LeRoi Jones rejected them for his Beat magazine, *Yugen*, something of which I reminded him long after he had transformed himself into Amiri Baraka. The homely, pastoral poems of northern New York that Douglas Angus admired no longer reared their bucolic heads.

I was thriving amid the sensory delights and alchemy of New York City. I was speaking, passing words and ideas with such renowned literary figures as Gore Vidal, William Saroyan, and Muriel Rukeyser. I met with young, up-and-coming writers like the street poet Jack Micheline, Jack Kerouac, and Ed Corley, who edited *Off-Broadway*, a theater review for which I also wrote. I met and interviewed Kenneth Rexroth at the Five Spot Café. At Cooper Union, I heard John Ciardi read his poems. I sat beside James Baldwin in a village restaurant; observed the great performer Jason Robards in a revival of O'Neill's *The Iceman Cometh*; sold books to Henry Fonda, Zero Mostel, Steve Allen, Walter Chrysler, and Carl Van Vechten; watched a white-bearded and frail Ezra Pound glance at his titles in the store I managed; spied John Steinbeck entering the Great Northern Hotel on West Fifty-Seventh Street; heard Leonard Bernstein conduct rehearsals at Carnegie Hall as a guest of Jack Fisher, the concertmaster. I visited Shirley Booth in her dressing room; I spoke with Rosemary Clooney often on the telephone; I knew dancers in the cast of the first *Candide*, including Frances Noble, and became great friends with Margaret Roy, a singer from that same great production. I touched the hands of Vera Zorina, Victor Mature, Sylvia Sydney, Carol Landis, and Anthony Perkins. I stood in my age, of my age, yet out of my age. Yet something was very wrong. A piece of life, of *my* life, was missing. As a youth I had been sure that, if I could just get the snows of northern New York off my shoulders and the grass off my tongue, I would be free and content. Life would open and welcome me. All would end happily. Things were happening; look at my successes. But there was a huge black hole in the center of my existence. It would take a while longer, another decade, to discover the missing pieces to the puzzle in order to complete the picture.

During the early years in which I worked at the Marboro bookstore, two supremely important people entered my life, and though both have since passed on to what I hope are just rewards, they each remain prominent in my memory, and their voices whisper at my ear every time I place a pen between two fingers. Where would I be today if their lives had never intertwined with mine? If their creative minds had never inspired me as a young poet? If I had ignored their sound advice or allowed their memory to become eroded by time and busyness? It is amazing how a single human being—particularly one to whom one is not related by blood—can activate the juices in a productive sense, can manipulate and direct a life, carving the raw amethyst into a stone worthy of being set into a ring.

Is it the wind at the corner as you turn? Is it predestination, or is it, as Thomas Hardy suggests, "crass chance"? Who knows? Not I. But we are gloriously thankful, deliriously indebted to whatever cause or sprite entangles our lives with others! The woman you speak to in the museum, perhaps out of curiosity, eventually becomes your wife. The man with whom you share a Greyhound seat while crossing America becomes your publisher, or perhaps your assassin. An accidental dial of the telephone may lead to the most bizarre events.

The small room in the brownstone on Morton Street into which I moved in 1957 was not much larger than six by ten feet. I was a tenacious young poet with a head start on success. One thin book was in my pocket, *The Hopeless Kill*. It had been published privately at the *Watertown Daily Times*—in the wee hours, in the dark upstairs rooms of what was then the paper's office on Stone Street. The city editor had done the job. Many years ago, the publisher of the paper, John B. Johnson, was to receive a citizens' award, and I was invited to give the keynote address at the SUNY presidents' annual conference. Mr. Johnson and I talked together afterward, and he informed me that he had been aware all along of what was going on upstairs in the dark at his paper's offices and that, in retrospect, he didn't mind at all.

Now it seems like a story from Sherwood Anderson's *Winesburg, Ohio*. Here is a poet with his own thin volume in his pocket, sitting in a cramped room, a ratty dresser nearly touching the cot-bed, at a window overlooking a typical New York back garden, eating an orange and a small hunk of white cheese. He's reading the French poets Paul Éluard and Guillaume Apollinaire. He's waiting to go downstairs to meet the eminent writer Willard Motley, a man who once seemed destined to be remembered among the all-time greats, but whose fame has since (and sadly) eroded. Motley was in New York City proofing his novel *Let No Man Write My Epitaph* for Random House. Somehow, he too discovered the available rooms in the house at 66 Morton Street, a fact I discovered when I came upon a letter on the hall table addressed to him. An audacious lad, I took that letter and pushed it under his door, along with a personal note, to which he kindly responded, inviting me to his equally tiny room for a jelly jar full of cheap Chianti. Within two years of our meeting, I was living and working in his house on the outskirts of Mexico City while he tried to write his fourth novel, a ragged but wonderful manuscript he left with me and which I still hope can find a publisher someday. He and I spent hours working through it, though not always while he was in the best frame of mind for writing. Nevertheless, it contains the spark of brilliance that made *Knock on Any Door* a masterful novel.

Willard taught me to write every single day, not to wait for an inspiration. Keep a journal, enter everything, then select and write. Observation was of the utmost importance for him, and memory was the enemy because it could easily delude in the present, could deceive, lie, or refuse to cough up the names and numbers, incidents and experiences. Don't trust memory, he'd insist. Keep a notebook. Eventually, I learned to prod the memory with postcards and photos, but I gave up the journal as the writing in it became maudlin, embarrassing, and best forgotten.

At the same time I was having these lush, rich chats with Willard—over wine in his room or tea in mine—I was studying at New York University under Louise Bogan. I consider her the most important lyric woman poet published since 1900. No matter what mode—poem, story, essay, letter . . . even e-mail—I am composing in, Ms. Bogan is never far from my thoughts. She taught me to edit *out* . . . rarely ever to edit in or to flesh out. Select, select, and select some more and then cut away the parts that weren't selected. This was important, but her other advice was perhaps even more to the point, and exactly what was most needed in my life and work. What on earth was I doing reading those French poets and Rilke, especially in translation? Read the Americans, she said. There were, and still are, great American voices, but do not get bogged down in the lyrical rhetoric of Whitman, the sentimentality of Benét, the stealing of Vachel Lindsay, and certainly not the apparent formlessness of Edgar Lee Masters. Cull from the past; cull from experience; do not ignore history or art; utilize what has passed before your eyes and heart and spirit. Exert discipline on your poems by attempting to create new forms if the old ones do not work for your voice. She helped me to shape my voice and gave me a better understanding of place than I'd had before. Know who you are, where you hail from, and have some idea of where you are plotting to go, your destination as a living human being. Carry no shame for your culture, your past, or yourself. She thought of herself as being "shanty Irish," and was proud of how she had overcome this stigma; and in her youth it truly *had* been a stigma, very similar to being an American Indian. Ms. Bogan (I still cannot write of her as "Louise") taught me, encouraged me, to look back, to look at the fields of home, the woods and hills, the chicory and owls, the berries of the sandlots, to listen to the voices that were continually speaking, their echoes surrounding us. She taught me elegance and eloquence in the execution of these garnered images; the snow on the shovel, not just the "cherry tree," the raindrop on the earlobe. Be elegant, but simple; remember that the ordinary in the hands of the master becomes masterful. Her teachings were not too far afield from the advice of Werner Beyer. I have written of my experience as a student of Louise Bogan many times elsewhere. I can sum it up here simply by saying that she was a guiding light in my program, my history, my own poetry. Like Beyer and Angus; like Rocco and Cigar; like Etta and Aunt Flo; like David and Midge before her . . . a savior, or at the least a beacon to my life.

When I was a guest of the Modern Language Association Conference in New York City in 1987, I had the good fortune to sit beside and to chat with Elizabeth Frank, who had received the Pulitzer Prize the previous year for her magnificent biography of Ms. Bogan. She appeared pleased to meet me, one of the great poet's former students. Among the other scholars who sat at the dais for this symposium on Bogan's lyric poetry was Ruth Limmer, who had completed Bogan's pasted-together autobiography, *Journey Around My Room*. The session opened with Ms. Bogan reciting several poems on tape, which allowed her ghost to enter the room. Her strength once more overpowered me; her elegance, shy but profound, engulfed me. I was carried back to the first night in her classroom, when she readily admitted that she was not going to teach us how to write poetry. She would correct our punctuation and grammar, and we should not expect more; if we did, "then go get your tuition back." Wisely, I did not go to the bursar's office for the tuition, but remained and studied.

The year of the MLA symposium was also the year that my volume of selected poetry, *Between Two Rivers*, was published. I gave Miss Limmer, who was Bogan's literary executrix, a signed copy. She looked surprised when I told her who I was. *Journey Around My Room* is indeed a mosaic of various writings by Ms. Bogan. It deals with her life as woman and artist, though it weaves and braids with joy and depression. She was a tragic woman in my mind for all her successes, poems, and awards. That book has served me as something of a model for my own writing here, just as her approach to poetry and her bearing in regard to life in general served me previously.

Ms. Bogan was in great demand on the reading/lecture circuit in those days. She frequently missed classes, but never canceled. We students were fortunate in her replacement or proctor. It was always the poet Donald Allen, editor of probably the most important and perhaps the first Beat anthology, *New American Poetry*, which remains a classic. Allen was in class the evening I was to present Ms. Bogan with my poem "Dead Letters Sent." Allen read it aloud to the class and then asked me to read it. Once class was finished, we walked to the subway together. He praised the poem and exclaimed that had he read it sooner, he would have included it in his anthology. It was too late. The book was with the typesetter. His statement was a great thrill anyway.

Louise Bogan brought me home, returned me to the snows and hills of northern New York. She, along with Willard Motley, shined much-needed light into that dark hole, the missing ingredient in my life that would allow me not only to live, but also finally to write in the way that I felt I could. They helped transform me from a student of poetry, capable of aping the work of others, but not yet in command of my own voice. Many of the poems in my collection, *Dead Letters Sent*, were produced under Bogan's direct guidance, particularly the title poem which she admired.

twenty-one

More People and Places

Paddy Chayefsky was a short stout man when I first met him in the Fifty-Seventh Street Marboro in 1960. Already he had received accolades and national attention for his film *The Goddess*; the TV dramas *Marty* and *The Catered Affair*; and his Broadway success, *Middle of the Night*, which he also adapted into a screenplay for a Hollywood film starring Fredric March and Kim Novak. He was about to receive enormous praise for another Broadway production, *The Tenth Man*. Paddy was born a Jew in New York in 1923, but despite this we shared many similarities (although not as many as Sarah would have believed). Even though we were not far apart in age, he became a father figure for me; perhaps it helped that by the time I met him, he was married and a biological father (though, strangely, I never met his family). He embraced the role of my mentor, at the same time allowing and encouraging my guidance in certain realms, particularly when it came to advising him on what to read.

Chayefsky blustered into the long, narrow shop out of the north wind, his dark overcoat upsetting books placed on the cash desk. He came off as cocky and arrogant, and yet his twinkling eyes belied meanness. When he spoke, it was in a near shout, a voice suited for command. Apparently, he had worked sufficient years in the theater that he had acquired a directorial attitude and well-trained vocal chords. He was Broadway's golden boy at that time. His plays and TV dramas were hugely successful, so he had a right to a boisterous, demanding personality. The opposite side of his character, off-stage, was that of May snow melting. (Budd Schulberg, like Chayefsky, had that same rough exterior, but his soul too was made of lark or hummingbird feathers.)

"I'm going to Russia for the State Department with other American writers on a cultural exchange," Paddy exclaimed. Something of a thrill was mixed with his businesslike gruffness. "I need to take a collection of American authors!" My astonished face met his absolutely honest eyes. "I don't mean Hemingway and the like. They know *him*." We spent an hour together, rattling off names and discussing various writers, though my memory fails to produce the exact names and titles after all these years. Surely, we must have discussed Truman Capote, Willard Motley, Jean Stafford, and William Faulkner, who was not terribly fashionable in literary circles at that precise moment, despite . . . or perhaps because of . . . winning the Nobel Prize. I know I would have suggested James Purdy's masterpiece, *Malcolm*. I met Purdy years later when both of us were living in Brooklyn Heights. We bumped into each other at a secondhand bookstore and became fast friends. In 1986 I copublished his poetry collection *Brooklyn Branding Parlor*, through my Contact/II Press. I also would certainly have advised Paddy to pack Shirley Jackson and Shirley Ann Grau's *The Black Prince*, which was enjoying a hearty success. And, of course, some Flannery O'Connor. The classics he must have already known . . . Hawthorne, Melville, James Cooper, Cather, Crane and Wharton . . . though I was never exactly sure. He was a graduate of City College of New York, a reputable college. What Paddy's major was, though, I have no inkling. It was obvious he knew few of the leading American authors of his time other than Hemingway's ex-pat gang, Steinbeck, and the playwrights . . . O'Neill, Miller, Williams, and so on. Thanks to my counsel, he appeared happy and relieved of a burden. With a handshake and a smile, he bombed out through the open door into the late winter afternoon and soon flew off to Russia. His figure disappeared from sight and mind, another demanding celebrity who knew no bounds in harassing a book clerk's brain and causing sore feet.

I had met many Hollywood actors . . . Ralph Bellamy and Henry Fonda, for example . . . who were of that nature; they would spend hours of your time browsing art books only to storm out of the shop without making a single purchase. Some of both the famed and the infamous were not always greeted with happiness and smiles in the Marboro. Usually the poets were more humane, understanding, and compassionate toward weary underpaid clerks. Muriel Rukeyser, who had just then published *One Life*, a biography of Wendell Willkie, was unfailingly warm and gentle, and always made time to speak about writing to this nosey poet. Many years later, after a reading of her work at the University of Buffalo, she recalled the bookshop and the many delightful chats we had. She had suffered a stroke recently and came to the stage with the help of a cane. Her poems were printed on very large plastic placards, for she was also going blind. Indeed, only a few months later she passed into literary history.

This meeting at UB with Rukeyser reminded me of Billie Holiday's last concert, at Randall Stadium in New York. I was there. She was led to the microphone, which she gripped for dear life. At the end of her performance, the great lady was again led off the stage to thunderous applause, even though drugs and the more mundane burdens of life itself had stolen much of her magical voice. America has produced many startling artists, artists who have borne pain and suffering of both body and soul that may not have been displayed on their countenances. Roy Marz's writings helped me to wear that mask early on and I don't know that I ever really took it off all the way.

Chayefsky returned from Russia a few months later and stopped into the store not long thereafter. We became acquaintances, then friends, and next I found myself in his employ. Once he was to go on a safari to Africa. He invited me to travel as his companion at his expense. I declined the invitation, partly because it had sounded more like a command. He could be difficult, and anyway, I was involved in a heated affair. At the time, he had been commissioned by Elizabeth Taylor to write a screenplay of the life of Edna St. Vincent Millay, in which Taylor, naturally, would star. We worked very hard on the script; Paddy diligently reporting each new scene to Miss Taylor. We finished, struggled over the title, came up with something, as I now recall, like *The Rose.* Upon receiving the script, Miss Taylor ignored the hard labor, even the inspired creativity, and brushed off the work; she, or some agent working for her, decided that Millay was not a subject worthy of her talents. Paddy and I were devastated, but got over it before too long. That business is not one that encourages long spells of moping, at least not if one wants to work again.

In March of 1962, I left to go to California with Wanda and ended up traveling through Mexico with her. I never saw or spoke with Paddy again. Occasionally, I take down from the bookshelf his volumes of plays and reread inscriptions like this one: "To Maurice—without whom I would have no leisure." Paddy has since died, but he left a rich legacy. The great American literary critic Edmund Wilson has written that Paddy Chayefsky was "cheap, conceited, and corny." Wilson heatedly disagreed with Paddy's ideas concerning Russia and Lenin. Personally, I did not find Paddy either cheap or corny; conceited, well, I'm not so sure. We must remember that Wilson was an upper-crust literary snob, even though he undoubtedly possessed a great mind. My friendship with Paddy was another Odysseus-Telemachus experience without the blood tie, and I shall always remember this remarkable man with affection and pride. His skill and glamour were contagious, offering me something I had always yearned for but considered unattainable.

The West Fifty-Seventh Street Marboro often seemed a literary soirée: the ambiance was breathtaking to us menial clerks—George, Nick, Charley, Mike, Ed, and I. We trembled in awe of the famous actors, writers, and painters who scurried in and out of the shop, but we were too intimidated to approach them. Ralph Soyer, who taught at the Art Students League, periodically walked our aisles. The Countess Maria von Trapp, whose life was portrayed in *The Sound of Music*, many a time leaned her Alpine-attired elbows on my desk. Katharine Hepburn came in on several evenings, but I was always off-duty, much to my chagrin. Sylvia Sidney came and went regularly with six or seven yapping poodles. She was sweet, but overly made-up; lipstick rather drooled from her wrinkled lips, and rouge clowned her cheeks. She was delighted that we remembered her Hollywood portrayals, and later, I was especially happy when, brought out of retirement, she received an Academy Award for *Summer Wishes, Winter Dreams*. It was not beyond imagination that she and Henry Fonda might appear together in the store as they had starred together in *The Trail of the Lonesome Pine*, the film for which she is best remembered.

Two other women of lesser prominence than Sidney and Hepburn also frequented the store. A certain Mrs. Anspacher, a most elegant lady up in years, struck up an acquaintance with me and would often take me to lunch. She once offered me her summer home in Connecticut, so that I could write away from the stress and bustle of city life. There were strings attached to this invitation that didn't really offend me, but rather shocked my youngish sensibilities. Mrs. Anspacher was very handsome; her physical beauty reminded me of Louise Bogan to a degree. She was very wealthy and always wore many large diamonds. Perhaps I missed a "golden opportunity" for patronage. Perhaps I missed out on being the role model for *Harold and Maude*. Later it was published that she had willed a sizable amount of money to the Joseph Papp Theater in memory and honor of her late husband, who had been something of a playwright and poet. Mrs. Anspacher recorded his verses as she channeled his spirit from the afterlife. She inscribed a copy of the published book to me.

Another woman, who popped into the shop late one afternoon in order to ask a question, was a "lady with a past." Born in Hungary, Mary Tarcai had been a young actress with considerable stage experience and a few minor television and film credits to her name in the mid-1950s, the time of McCarthy's terrible and tragic witch hunts. She and her husband, a TV producer, had been named as communist sympathizers because of their association with the Actors' Laboratory Theatre in Los Angeles in the late 1940s. Mary certainly had political ideas and ideals, but who didn't? To breathe in America is political, as the bromide goes. I have no reason to believe then, or to consider now, that Mary was a Communist. The subject never came up in any of our conversations. Nor did she ever introduce me to friends who might be "red" or even "pink." But the scandal had ruined her fledgling film career, and she and her husband had returned to New York City. He resumed production of TV dramas such as *Cain's Hundred*; Mary opened a drama studio on West Fifty-Sixth Street across from the stage door of the New York State Theater, now located at Lincoln Center. Her talents and generosity were phenomenal and widely known. A strict coach, and one who dug into the very marrow of an actor's passion, she found the core of your being. She insisted that her students be working in a Broadway show, a film, a TV series, or at least singing or dancing in a club or on the concert stage. Among her students were Tina Louise (*God's Little Acre* and *Gilligan's Island*), Gower Champion (dancer/choreographer of many hit Broadway musicals), and Charlotte Rae (famous later in her career for *The Facts of Life*). At that time in New York City there were many dramatic coaches. Mary certainly ranked at the top along with Stella Adler and Uta Hagen.

It did not take many visits for Mary to strike up a friendship with me. Her warmth and creativity overwhelmed me. Her jubilant, bubbling, intellectually stimulating, and pointed conversation was intoxicating. She nearly always dressed in black or dark purple. I thought she was a gypsy (we still used that term back then, alas), not a Hungarian Jew. She seemed a swirl of shawls and scarves. A tall, pale woman, she possessed the long, slim fingers of a pianist. She had a large circle of important show-business friends, and the parties in her lavish apartment glittered with stellar names of Broadway and Hollywood. This apartment on West Seventy-Second Street was just around the corner from the famous Dakota, where I visited writers and the actor Robert Ryan from time to time. The grand galas at Mary's were intimidating for a young country man like myself, no matter how much sophistication I thought I had gained during my years in the city. I was usually speechless and terrified of so much as shaking hands with the famous. Mary, a true "Mother Spirit, Mother Courage," insisted that I should teach a course at her school to be called "The History of Drama from the Greeks to Tennessee Williams." I taught this course with much pleasure for two years until I left for Mexico in 1962. Mary introduced me to the Broadway and film producer Robert Fryer and the brilliant actor José Ferrer, whom I had seen many years before on Broadway in a production of Shakespeare's *Othello* starring Paul Robeson. Both Fryer and Ferrer were constantly on the lookout for fresh properties to stage. Mary, naturally, thought I should write a play for them. I read newly published novels and short-story collections and made several suggestions, none of which were pursued, as far as I know. Thinking back now, I can be sure that I pushed Faulkner's novel *Light in August* as a potential play. Years later I was asked to write a libretto for an opera by Tom Briccetti to celebrate the opening of a new civic center in Florida. I again offered *Light in August*, which was summarily dismissed as being too expensive. Tom and I lost the commission, though he did set several of my poems to music for the flute. After I returned from Mexico, I never had the joy of Mary's company again; I never again saw her purple shawls, her smiles, or heard her staccato laughter. One of us disappeared.

The Marboro shop on Fifty-Seventh Street was a cornucopia and kaleidoscope of adventure and fantasy, an encyclopedia of dreams and wishes. My time there was a very rich six years in the life of a budding poet. Of the thousands of people who entered through its doors in those years—the hundreds of celebrities like Eve Merriam and Anthony Perkins (who was always trying to borrow a tea bag and rarely bought whichever cookbook he stood for hours reading, probably memorizing the recipes), the actors, the poets, the painters, the musicians, the playwrights, the wealthy and important, and the handful who exerted some influence or offered a thumbnail of advice—one man stands out fondly in my memory as the most vivid and extraordinary individual who distinctively affected my writing, a unique literary figure of little fame but a long career, a figure who much influenced my youthful creativity and intellect: Samuel Loveman. Altruistic, he was a walking library card file, the author of only one collection of poetry, now long, long out of print, *The Hermaphrodite and Other Poems*. He did publish several other books, editing *Twenty-One Letters of Ambrose Bierce* and *A Round-Table in Poictesme*, a collection of essays on James Branch Cabell. He was also a lifelong aficionado and critic of the fantasy writer H. P. Lovecraft. As a young poet, he was on most intimate of terms with Hart Crane.

Loveman shuffled into the Fifty-Seventh Street store one cold winter day, his large nose fiery red, his cheeks burning from the zero-degree temperature. A tatty hat topped his balding head framed by gray-white hair. He wore baggy trousers that ruffled at the ankles, cracked shoes desperately in need of polish, and fogged glasses. Short and slightly round-shouldered, he stooped over the book counters, poked around the shelves approvingly, and passed out the door with a hand wave and a mumbled thank-you. He returned the next day to bargain for multiple copies of a certain collection of poetry that he'd spied on the table the day before. Immediately, we pushed aside the bargaining and delved into the world of poets and poems. He spoke of his own secondhand bookstore down in the West Village on Sullivan Street and said that I must visit some evening, which I soon did. It was usually inhabited by minor, mostly unknown writers. Soon invitations came to visit his apartment on upper Second Avenue over "the sign of the fish." Through the years, I returned again and again to his home, which seemed to be built on books. Except in the extremely large kitchen, piles of books had consumed the seven-room flat. He lived in the kitchen, where there was a cot near the stove, a writing table near the sink, a floor lamp for light, and a bowl of fruit for refreshment. Only the indomitable Helen Adam, in her tiny apartment on East Eighty-Second Street, which she shared with her sister Patricia, had (in my experience, anyway) such a huge and diverse collection of books assembled in such unusual places . . . in the oven, as legs for the dining table, and so on. Sam Loveman was and continues to be precious. I shall never forget him or the realms of books through which he guided me, all the while scattering fairy dust along the way. There was never sufficient time of an evening to explore all that his literal rooms and the figurative rooms of his mind encompassed, but the exploration helped to satisfy the curiosity of a book-obsessed youth.

Sam Loveman's generosity knew no bounds. He attempted to have my poems published by his editor friends; he introduced me to living and dead authors whom I probably would not otherwise have met; he praised my work, offering substantial criticism of early poems; he offered to write the introduction to *Dead Letters Sent*, in which he promised a healthy and successful writing career. Sam died in August 1976, the same year that Walter Lowenfels (another helpful writer-editor) and Louis Ginsberg (Allen's father and an accomplished poet in his own right) passed. I have affectionately and gratefully written of Sam many times in numerous publications and in a long poem concerning the parallels he alleged to exist between my poetry and that of Hart Crane. The latter was a fallacy: I have never been influenced by Crane, nor can I truthfully say I enjoyed his work, though I have nevertheless produced an entire manuscript of poems about him. Louise Bogan told me that she had yet to finish *The Bridge* and did not feel that she had a strong understanding of its intention and meaning. Sam died alone in a New York City hospital with only a nurse and the executor of his will at hand. I had visited him only a day or so before his last breath. Totally blind and heavily medicated, he hallucinated that I was Hart Crane and cursed me for desiring fame.

The rooming house at 66 Morton Street offered many good times and new friends as well. During the time I lived there, I met some crazy, weird, delightfully bohemian people, as well as others of a more serious . . . though not totally dreamless . . . nature. I have forgotten their names, if indeed I ever knew them. I'm only left with behaviors and characteristic eccentricities, such as the lady who wept and screamed all night and awoke fresh and beautiful in the morning as though she had stepped out of a Hollywood musical. Or the young woman who strolled through the cafes handing out red roses to young lovers; wearing only a silken slip, she wafted the scent of fine brandy, and Marie, our building's super, couldn't accept that she was an African American woman. With a perspective as firm and inflexible as Sarah's, Marie insisted that the woman *surely* must have been something more exotic than that! People often came and went in the middle of the night at the Morton Street rooming house. You'd meet and chat with them outside the shower room one morning, and then that afternoon see them hurrying down the street, suitcase in hand. Marie would be chasing behind, screaming for rent.

One person I remember well was a young African American student of journalism named Robert C. Maynard. He and his wife also lived in a large dank rooming house, not at 66 Morton but at Barrow and Fourth. Their single room had a sink and a hot plate, and the bathroom was down a long, dark hallway. Many a night we sat on their stoop and drank cheap wine and read the poems of Edna St. Vincent Millay until dawn. Someone might hum a bar of Mozart, and we'd hold a lively discussion about Shaw's criticism of Beethoven, applaud the current revival of Lorca's *Blood Wedding*, or dissect the politics of the moment, the drug scene around the corner at Sheridan Square, the jazz at the local club, or whatever else struck our curious fancy. Those were great nights and great dawns. Then we'd dally off to work or school, happy with the near darkness, the street patter of feet, the car horns, and the color of our neighborhood. We hoped the village tourists would take us for bohemians.

Even though we typed our papers on manual typewriters, and there were no microwave ovens, Burger Kings, or Pizza Huts, we had time to write and talk and dream. We survived on Spam and hard rolls with crackling crusts. Hamburgers were rare, and steak was beyond our comprehension, let alone suits from Alexander's or Macy's. Books were bought secondhand from the shop on Sheridan; with only the rarest of exceptions that were dependent on knowing someone who owed a favor, plays were strictly off-Broadway. Who cared? We were young; we had Bach, O'Neill, Miller, and Mistral. We had poetry readings in the cafes, the Museum of Modern Art, the Met. We could watch Wright erect the Guggenheim on Fifth Avenue; we had evenings with guitars in Washington Square. There were forbidden moonlight swims in the pool behind the Varick Street library (where I gave my first public reading). We had every right to fancy ourselves poets, artists, journalists, young lovers, and cosmopolitan intellects. We were the eggheads, an expression now long out of fashion. We sought other heads equal to our own. George Bernard Shaw was an icon. Truman Capote was revered, as were Carson McCullers and Federico García Lorca. We were poor but elegant snobs, poor as the proverbial church mouse, naked as the emperor, colorful as Joseph's coat. We wanted for nothing, and nothing was wanting. Spam and peanut butter every night was fine as long as there was a ninety-cent bottle of red wine with which to wash it down. And we argued over the quality of those cheap wines from Spain! We ate pans of macaroni doused with oleo and parsley. We "stooped" the Village and sneered at the tourists who strolled by rubbernecking our lives.

One day my two friends announced that they were moving to a larger apartment in Brooklyn Heights, near Crane's glorious, enigmatic, mysterious bridge. I did manage one trek by subway to their new place. Then they vanished, and Wanda and I disappeared out west and into Mexico. The next time I saw Robert C. Maynard he was guesting on the David Brinkley Sunday morning show. He had become editor and publisher of the *Oakland Tribune*, and was enjoying prestige and obviously a fine salary. He no longer wore sweaters missing the elbows, but a jacket and tie. I suspected that he no longer slouched along the street, for there he sat, proud and straight in a director's chair, discussing the political problems of the world with important people. I was so proud of him and wondered if he remembered my poems. When I read his obituary in 1993, I was deeply saddened at his passing from the world at far too young an age.

Through the years, many of my fellow workers at Marboro and acquaintances from the West Village have revisited me from the TV screen. Not only Bob Maynard and Mike Hadge, but also Allan Miller, whose face I've seen looking back at me while watching *Soap* or *Nero Wolfe* or any number of other shows in which he played supporting parts. Alice Ghostley went on to considerable fame; we had known the actor G. Wood by his given name of George long before he played the psychiatrist in *Harold and Maude*, among other parts. What a wonderful thing television is for me! It rings out the new and rings back the old, a veritable storehouse of memories. I think that the friends and students who have fed at my kitchen table through the years must think me daffy as I go on about the old friends from my youth who occasionally pass across the screen. They suspect my credibility and patronize my memory as though I had imagined these noted people, conjured them out of fantasy.

The joys and richness of that bohemian life did not translate into a great deal of success at the literary life for me, though, and I felt the old urge to roam once again. I left New York in the early 1960s and lived for a while in Mexico, where I worked as a secretary to Willard Motley for over a year. From there I moved on to the U.S. Virgin Islands, where I met Tram Combs, the poet who introduced me to Florence Williams, widow of William Carlos Williams. Though aging, Mrs. Williams was a real charmer. It was a sheer delight to meet her, press her hand, and talk with her. In Charlotte Amalie, I lived in Cha Cha Town near the Russian mansion, then in tatters and rubble, and among the summer homes of many wealthy continentals. Herman Wouk also lived and wrote there on the island. One of his novels, *The Carnival*, deals with St. Thomas and Charlotte Amalie.

In May 1966 I flew from the Islands to Chicago, where I took a job with the *Chicago Sun-Times*. For exactly one year, I wrote obituaries. Having discovered Chicago to be cold, unfriendly, and provincial, I proceeded to Greyhound back to Brooklyn Heights, where I found a one-room studio on the fifth floor of an old brownstone at 62 Clark Street for sixty-five dollars a month. I filled the room with bright colors . . . magenta, cobalt, acid greens, melon, and lemon, all the colors I had grown to love in Mexico and the Caribbean. Moving only once, into the brownstone next door, I would end up living in Brooklyn for the next twenty years, until I was hired as a poet-in-residence at North Country Community College and gradually began moving back to my Adirondack homeland, albeit with a fair number of temporary detours to Oklahoma, British Columbia, and so on.

It was around 1970 when I became involved in owning some apartments in Chicago with a longstanding friend, Joaquin Perez. Joaquin . . . better known as Quino . . . was a merchant mariner and consequently out of Chicago on the high seas much of the time. I was elected to perform the landlord duties: to collect rent before paychecks got spent at the local taverns, to exterminate cockroaches, to paint walls, to buy hot-water heaters, to mow lawns, to solve arguments or disputes among the buildings' tenants, and naturally, to keep the five apartments rented. The two buildings were nestled within a blue-collar neighborhood that was undergoing some demographic changes. Hispanics were gradually moving in, and guitars, cha-cha-cha, and the rhythms of salsa music colored the air.

twenty-two

Native Consciousness

In my role as landlord and super, I flew to Chicago once a month. On one of my trips to the Windy City, I found myself without a book for the flight home and made a serendipitous purchase at the La Guardia airport newsstand: Mari Sandoz's *Cheyenne Autumn*, an American epic. Now, tattered and well thumbed, the same copy remains near at hand on the bookshelf beside my writing desk, and within its leaves rests a postcard depicting the young, brash, notoriously confident (to the point of possible mental disorder) George Armstrong Custer. The photo was taken of the young general a year before his demise in 1876 at Little Big Horn. The card had been sent by my good friend Frank Parman, who sadly never published the history of Oklahoma that he carried around in his mind like a burden and that would have made a gigantic and authentic book. *Cheyenne Autumn* is the history of 278 Northern Cheyenne men, women, and children who, despite the extreme duress of winter, broke out of their Fort Robinson, Nebraska, prison in 1878 to escape north to their homelands on the Yellowstone River in Montana. They had been ravaged in the freezing barracks by starvation, acute illness, hopelessness, loss of spirit, and their lost freedom, and by the false promises of the government that they might be allowed to return home. Under the bitterest of conditions they fled the fort, and under heavy army cavalry fire they crawled north across the plains in biting winds. Nearly half of these Cheyenne died from gunfire or exposure. Theirs was truly an American epic; their band was led by two mighty and sensitive chiefs, Little Wolf and Dull Knife. Truly, tears stained my cheeks throughout the flight, and those tears have continued to fall through the years, especially as I sit in Saranac Lake, observing the winds of March whip a snowstorm before my eyes, reminding me of the Cheyennes' heroic escape and their horrendous march home under the most grueling conditions.

Cheyenne Autumn led me to many other books by Mari Sandoz: *Old Jules*; *The Battle of the Little Bighorn*; *The Buffalo Hunters*; *The Beaver Men: Spearheads of Empire*; *Love Song to the Plains*; and her masterpiece, *Crazy Horse*, the biography of the great Lakota leader, a man of mystery but also a man of heroic proportions. Furthermore, reading her work led me on to other books, histories concerned with the Cheyenne, especially the Southern Cheyenne now at home in Western Oklahoma. In *Cheyenne Autumn*, Sandoz introduces a young Cheyenne woman, Monahsetah, and her son, Yellow Swallow, with the strong suggestion that this sickly lad had been fathered by Custer during his winter campaign against the Cheyenne in 1869, notable for Custer's dawn attack upon a peaceful band of Cheyenne under the leadership of Black Kettle. I spent the next five years researching this allegation with the intent of writing Monahsetah's biography and including proof that Custer sired the young Yellow Swallow, who died on the journey north to Nebraska. I wrote the book essay by essay, but when it was nearly complete I abandoned my labors, having been unable locate the essential and definitive facts. I came back to his story decades later, only after realizing that the truth of the situation was less a matter of historical facts than of understanding who had the voice with which to tell the story. Monahsetah was just the first of many Native voices to whom I would lend my fingers and my mouth in order for their stories to be told. In the process of doing so, I also learned to tell the part of my own story that was distinctly Native, distinctly Mohawk.

If both Werner Beyer and Louise Bogan had pointed to the road home, then surely Mari Sandoz, whom I never had the good fortune to meet, produced the vehicle in which to ride there. The flight from New York to Chicago, the reading of that epic (as valid as any ancient Greek tragedy or martyrdom of Christians slaughtered in the Roman Coliseum), the tears that have remained, their stain on my cheeks, all brought me home. Truly it was time as a poet to forget Ransom, Eliot, Frost, Williams, Jeffers, and even Bogan, and become myself. The dark was lifting, but the abyss I had been facing all my life was close, its great hole filling with history, culture, past deprivation, loneness, pain, and history. I had dug into all that with a fine lyric spade that would open veins of purple blood, songs aching for remembrance. I was releasing the collective memory, to misquote Carl Jung, of thousands of years of Native glory and survival, as well as the horror and brutality of the invasion and division by conquistadores who were not simpatico with any man or woman of copper skin, with any who hung a feather at the ear or danced upon the drum of earth. The Native societies were of the utmost sophistication, with workable and working governments, educational systems, and scientific minds, and the ceremonial rituals and profound spirituality of their enduring religions. The greedy invaders of these lands that existed "on a turtle's back" had not yet conceived such civilizations. Thousands of years of prayer, song, and story were the central pole of the various and magnificent cultures that were soon nearly to perish from the human collective memory despite the "usefulness" of the vanishing race. The invader was not totally successful in wiping out, extinguishing, these peoples. Mari Sandoz, among others, kept them alive, and the people took nourishment and reproduced. The process is neither complete nor easy nor guaranteed to succeed, but indigenous peoples are once more gaining strength and population, pride and dignity about who they were and who they are.

Now that I rode in a new vehicle home, I consumed a new alphabet and language, new words, paragraphs, books, tomes, and rites. I did not write in isolation but in an age marked by uprisings among the peoples who had been pushed down for centuries. The year 1969 saw the start of the occupation of Alcatraz Island by the "Indians of All Tribes" group; this action wouldn't end until eighteen months later when the federal government forcibly removed the occupiers. In 1973, the tragic confrontation broke out near Pine Ridge at Wounded Knee. Again, people were murdered, and some simply disappeared forever from human eyes. Others again were forced into jails, freedom and spirit denied.

I was not present at Wounded Knee in the church, shelled by government bullets, because I had a heart attack that June; nevertheless, my mind and spirit took a position in that church and eventually inspired me to write a Ghost Dance song that I called "I Am the Sun." When I regained a semblance of health, I returned north to the St. Lawrence River Valley . . . to Akwesasne, the St. Regis Reservation, the home of the Mohawks, the eastern branch of the Haudenosaunee . . . in order to work with the various minds and hands producing the important journal *Akwesasne Notes*. At that time, it was edited by Jerry Gamble, a Jewish man of excellent mind and intelligence, who had been adopted into the Mohawk Nation because of his depth of concern, his knowledge, and his labors on behalf of not only Mohawks and Iroquois, but also Native people across North America. It was while living in Nation House that I composed the poems for *Dancing Back Strong the Nation*, which would come out in 1979 at the same time as "I Am the Sun." I was sleeping in a room belonging to Mohawk poet Alex (Karoniaktahke) Jacobs, who was off attending university in Canada at the time. Peter Blue Cloud . . . poet, trickster, storyteller, editor, and dearly missed friend . . . was then poetry editor of *Akwesasne Notes*. Daniel Thompson, poet and artist, was also there sharing mugs of Indian tea with me. I helped Peter sort out the poems to be printed in *Notes*. I wrote bits and pieces of book reviews. Generally, I tried to make myself useful when I wasn't working on my poems. *North: Poems of Home* had already appeared via *Blue Cloud Quarterly* under the editorship of Brother Benet Tvedten, who was making a tremendous impact on Native and American literature (I'm not sure that there really is a division between the two, especially if one thinks, as I now do, that American history is Native history and vice versa). Brother Benet was printing chapbook after chapbook of Native writers . . . at huge financial losses, I'm sure. Wendy Rose, Duane Niatum, the songs of Buffy Sainte-Marie, and so on; he was making visible what was then utterly invisible.

Sandoz watered seeds of history in my thinking that my father had planted. History itself had planted seeds, some of which were weeds that needed hoeing and pruning. Over years of reading Sandoz, her ideas led me from studies of the Cheyenne and the Lakota to my own Iroquois. I consulted with my Aunt Jennie, and she explained the Parker familial connection to me; we were related to the famous Seneca leaders, though no one in recent time had pursued this blood tie. My mother seemed either ignorant of it, or simply had no interest, no concern; she refused to speak of it. As my father had died in 1957, it was impossible for me to speak with him. But Aunt Jennie, the family historian, holds in her possession a very old Bible, which, honestly, I have not seen for years. It contains births and deaths covering many, many decades. The Jefferson County Historical Museum also contains a decent archive.

I knew stories, but I did not know history. Consequently, I began asking questions, listening, and reading. Dan Thompson and Ray (Tehanetorens) and John Fadden offered many answers. I read Arthur Parker and Lewis Henry Morgan and studied how the people of the Long House, the Haudenosaunee, formed our sophisticated culture; how government was created, mainly through the good message of the Peacemaker, Deganawidah. I made a study of the creation story and contemplated the mysteries, the magic, or medicine of these everlasting stories, which, indeed, are a narrative history of the Iroquois. The more I listened and read and thoughtfully considered, the more I observed and understood. Slowly my father's wisdom, his thoughts, and his stories began to make intelligent sense, as did his reasoning behind why or why not to do something. His code of life became evident; his humanism was clear; his respect for the smallest or largest creature became understandable. I fully understood, for example, why food should not be wasted; it is the flesh of a thing once living that has given up life that we . . . that I . . . may live in good health. Not only were the scales falling from my sight, but the darkness of ignorance slowly receded like the tides I had seen in Mexico and the Caribbean. As a boy I had always talked with trees, particularly the black willow; with fish, especially rainbow trout, which swam in the creek that flowed by my father's house; with birds, specifically the hawk, the messenger to the spirit world. Hawk became my fetish, as did the woodchuck. As an adolescent I witnessed a woodchuck's death in the green fields of spring, watching as others, who prized its tail to swing from a hat's brim, killed it purely for an ornament. This, my father taught, was wrong.

Things somehow began to fit in place, such as Bogan's and Beyer's suggestions that I needed to go home out of the darkness, the abyss. Peter Blue

Cloud often advised me to get out of the city, New York, and go north where real life was happening. Even the Cheyenne poet Lance Henson said, on visiting me in New York City, that he couldn't understand how any self-respecting Mohawk could live in a place like Brooklyn, not failing to mention that many of Manhattan's structures of high steel and iron were erected by Iroquois men, risking their lives for buildings they would never be allowed to inhabit.

Barbara Cameron (Lakota), Randy Burns (Paiute), and Sharol Graves (Crow) were three young Native students I met in San Francisco through a newspaper advertisement after my time at Akwesasne. Barbara was a writer, Randy was heading toward a law degree, and Sharol was both an artist and dancer. Three young, beautiful people centered in their cultures, eager to contribute, to give back to their cultures as they had been gifted with so much. We met and a world opened, pervaded by a prism of light and color. Barb and Sharol were students at Mills College; Randy was at San Francisco State, studying at that time with Paula Gunn Allen. The three had a radio program called Red Voices on the KPOO radio station. I read poems with them over the air many times. Randy introduced me to Paula at lunch on campus. I had been publishing poems in *Akwesasne Notes*, and Walter Lowenfels had published a poem of mine that Alex Jacobs had sent to him in his seminal anthology, *From the Belly of the Shark*, which came out around the time of Wounded Knee. As a result, Paula had some idea who I was, and we formed a friendship. Paula and her sister, Carol Lee Sanchez, introduced me to many writers in the Bay Area and, later, in the Albuquerque region, mostly Native writers.

In those days there weren't that many Native writers who were published. We were friends and helped each other by suggesting publications and readings. We shared what little was out there. Many a time a mug of coffee was all we received for a half-hour reading of our poems. Honorariums were insignificantly small. We were excited, thrilled, just to stand at a podium with an audience, its collective head bent in concentration on our songs and chants, our stories and histories. I am greatly indebted to Barbara, Randy, Sharol, and of course Paula. I had entered a community where I belonged. The feeling of being a real poet was invigorating. Apart from being published, I was in a circle, a sacred circle of life with like kind, my own kind, Native poets. I was no more the loner, the outlaw, nor even the delinquent.

Wendy Rose, her husband Arthur Murata, and I became three peas in a pod. I thought of her as the "Little Sister." In turn she referred to me as her "Big Brother." Considerable years separate us in age, and I am forever thankful that Wendy didn't refer to me as "Father." As time went on, I was fortunate to meet other writers with whom I became good if not fast friends: Janet Campbell-Hale, Mary Tall Mountain, Duane Niatum, Joseph Bruchac, Diane Burns, Joy Harjo,

Linda Hogan, Diane Decorah, Geary Hobson, Lance Henson . . . all Native writers. I enjoyed their beauty and talents. To this moment I hold these good people, all powerful writers, in a good light, in high regard, and I am utterly thankful that they entered my life. If any of my contemporaries have an influence on my work, Simon Ortiz and Leslie Marmon Silko certainly hold me in the palms of their hands. Their poems and songs, their rhythms and metaphors, their ideas, were strong inducements to my own spirit and a constant inspiration. They became heroes, and I was nearly tongue-tied when we first met to share talk and stories. I was absolutely excited by Wendy's lyric voice and also by Peter Blue Cloud's vision. I was deeply impressed with Peter's study of the river spirit, of the ripening and flight of thc milkwccd pod. These two writers cannot but leave at least a shadow on the poetry in English of this time. Duane Niatum and Geary Hobson, longstanding warm friends, gave me incredible support, and to this moment I feel guilty for never having given back a fair measure of what they offered me. Many contemporary poets have loaned me their hand, and certainly their written words, or have helped me to develop and maintain faith in my work during some very dark hours. I am obliged never to forget Daniel (Rokwaho) Thompson, artist, poet, and thinker, who shared his thoughts late into the summer night over many mugs of coffee and billows of cigarette smoke (and occasionally also in wintertime letters).

Four non-Native writers have persuaded my pen and brain over the years since the awakening of my consciousness, and they too are heroes: Jim Ruppert, Rochelle Ratner, Michael Castro, and the huggable "Beaver," Jerry Rothenberg. I desired their approval so much. Hopefully, I have gained it.

Hundreds of other people over the decades have touched and colored my life and writing, and I am grateful and also a better person for their ceremonies, their care, and the intellectual relationships we have had and, with many, that we still have. What would my erratic life have amounted to without those pillars of friendship, guidance, and strength, "the kindness of strangers" that Blanche DuBois relies upon so famously. I am little more than a collection, a collage, of their ideas and images; their faith and spirit have led me to emulate them as I once wished to emulate Gerard Manley Hopkins, Robinson Jeffers, and, yes, even William Wordsworth.

I have often spoken of the fact that the house cats who have shared my life in recent decades have tempered my anger and rage. Neither Sula nor the Queen would tolerate violence, and I have been of a violent, passionate nature for most of my life. Nothing was gray. Most people would think it idiotic to believe that a cat could lead you to self- awareness where many a trained therapist had failed, where parents or a succession of friends might not have succeeded, but we learn from listening. The bee teaches, the river teaches, the sun and the moon teach, humans teach, and we in turn consider, digest, separate, and gain self-knowledge by teaching ourselves; if we are fortunate, we come to find our state of "bliss," as Joseph Campbell would say. Listening to those cats as they refused to abide my self-righteousness helped me learn that we are obliged to be part of a community, an active member of society. Creating poetry and my lifelong friends have opened a crack or a link in the community circle; they have allowed me to enter and find a useful place.

This is the magic of life: the touching of hands to minds. Mystery abounds: it is on each elm leaf, each bear claw, each petal of each trillium; on the bones of our ancestors and in each drop of sperm, in each ovum, of all species. The mystery of creation: should we ever discover its truth, we will lose interest and die of ennui. This is why we continue seeking the new hand, why we take another hike into the mountains, a canoe trip down the river, read one more poem, or listen to another story. To touch into this great mystery . . . to study the mountain or river spirit, as Peter Blue Cloud might suggest . . . is life. Only the Creator is perfect; only the Creator makes no mistakes. Only the Creator . . . or as Paula Gunn Allen has written, "the Creatrix" . . . knows what is at the center of that mystery. In the quest for vision, the poet is there at the edge of the stand of maples, at the precipice above the stone quarry, at the peak of the mountain. Poetry is the richness and magic of imagination. We do not live to our fullest potential without it. Not university degrees, nor the counting house, nor the bank deposit can ever show the open link into the center of mystery, of life. Watch a milkweed seed's flight, or that of the dandelion's fluff; observe the butterfly shake out of its cocoon or the frog drop its tadpole tail and fins. We are rounding the circle; the ceremony is green; the song vibrates; the wolf is not extinct; the story continues; the poem is yet to be dotted with the finality of a period; spirit is strong; the leg and hand remain firm; and the memory is vivid, rich, luxuriant with the details of too many stories, of stories too long to relate here and now at this moment.

Many years ago a fine young poet-editor, Jason Shinder, invited me to submit some new poems for an anthology Harcourt Brace Jovanovich was to publish. The collection was titled *More Light: Father & Daughter Poems, a Twentieth-Century American Selection*. Shinder extended the definition of father and daughter. I have not sired a biological daughter or son, yet he accepted a poem from my persona book, *Tekonwatonti: Molly Brant*, a poem in Molly's voice addressing the father of the United States, George Washington, who was known to Iroquois people as "Town Destroyer." Molly is asking that the father of the new country allow the people of the Iroquois their culture, and that he not forget where the founders discovered the forms of the American government, which was based on the "good message" of the Peacemaker, Deganawidah. Naturally, I was quite pleased to be included in this important book, which contained poems not only by many living friends and passing acquaintances, but also by some of the very poets who had in one way or another influenced or touched my early work: T. S. Eliot, Muriel Rukeyser, Laura (Jackson) Riding, Amiri Baraka, Audre Lorde, Marilyn Hacker, and even John Crowe Ransom. What a surprise, a sheer delight! I have always held that revenge is coated not with cane sugar but with the traditional natural sweetener, maple syrup. Figuratively, I danced around the painted war post. I sang and again and again profusely thanked Louise Bogan, Werner Beyer, Douglas Angus, and all the others who gave me support and helped rekindle my faith in my own creative powers. And, yes, I thanked both Ransom and Marz again for the huge part they played in my development. Without their doubts to spur me on, I might have become a business major as my father advised in order to help stay hunger from the door.

We are rounding the circle; the ceremony is green; the links of the circle have been formed by so many hands and minds. When I left Butler University in 1956, Werner Beyer said I had been a wild weed that changed into a flower. I hope he was thinking of the blood-red trillium of the northern woods and the Adirondack Mountains, endangered but resilient. The sacred circle of life, the intersection of all the mathematical points, is coming together: the roundness of the whole, the fullness of life for which I am very thankful.

Adowe.

Coda

On May 21, 1995, St. Lawrence University bestowed an honorary degree upon my name and career, Doctorate of Literature . . . with all the rights and privileges, as Dr. Patti McGill Peterson, president of the university, proclaimed while I was being hooded in red, brown, and white. College was finished for me at that moment, at least as a student . . . I still taught for another sixteen years. But I was thrilled, perhaps more so than I would have been were I being knighted by the Queen of England or receiving the Nobel Prize . . . though I wouldn't mind finding out, if only for the sake of comparison.

I was shocked to receive a letter a couple of years ago notifying me that I was to be inducted into the New York State Writers Hall of Fame. My initial reaction was "Do they have the right person?" I was truly flabbergasted. It can't be true, they must have made a mistake. Not that it doesn't please me . . . it does so quite greatly, but I never expected this kind of thing. And when you look and see the names that are there . . . Herman Melville, Toni Morrison . . . people whom I've admired most of my writing life and now my name is beside theirs, I almost feel like that's immoral. I've cried a few times. It's something like a dream. I used to have these dreams where I flew over the stage of a Broadway theater, and as I flew the audience would clap. And I would think, "Hey! That means I'm going to be famous!" Or I'd be climbing up the walls of a huge building and there would always be people looking up and wondering when I was going to fall. And I still have those dreams. And I know they relate to my art, my writing. They have to.

I sat at the induction ceremony with two of my former students . . . now dear friends . . . on a spring day in New York in 2014, hearing kind words said about me and my work. I was barely there, though; I was talking with my father in my head the whole time, wondering what he'd say if he could hear these words, this notion that someone thought I was good enough to share a place with authors he himself might even have read, much less heard about.

What would my dad say? I journeyed in Mexico; I have flown to the Caribbean and South America and Europe. I have lived and taught in New York City, California, Oklahoma. I have even taught in British Columbia. I've been translated into French and German and Russian and Hungarian. What would he say? Unbelievable. A year before he died, sitting at the kitchen table, he wept, his face in his arms. I asked him why he was crying. His reply was that he feared for me: that I was effete, that I would not make it. That was in 1957. What would he say?

What happened to the man in the woods holding Happy on a rope? He is in my nightmares. Where did the young actor go who placed his hand over my mouth that terrifying night in the Alex Bay Theater? He is in my nightmares. How did that man in Louisiana fare after that shattering experience? He haunts my nightmares. They all walk in the angry rain and, unfortunately, they may still walk in that rain beside me.

What is truth? What is reality? What is verisimilitude? What is virtue? What is sin and who the sinner? . . . the child, the boy, the youth, or the man whose hand reached out in the dark to touch, to change forever, to soil the flesh and the spirit and the mind of innocence, the wildflower blowing in the breeze, the chicory, blue and pure, at the edge of the road though near the gulch, the gutter.

Dates are rarely used in this brief account of the first half . . . plus a bit . . . of my life, but I have sought as much truth as possible in remembering it here. The memory is good, clear, helped by the nightmares. There are times when memory can and will play tricks on the fingers tapping the keyboard of a machine, but always the nightmare is there to keep the mind, the recollections straight.

Oh my father, you should have kept your son at thy side in thy house of labor. Oh my mother you should not have explained the flaw. Oh my schoolmates, Rocco and Cigar, you should not have tempted me to revolution. Oh Joe, my friend, my friend, I have abandoned you. David, what can I say? I never reached Mexico that first time, but I made it in 1962 with Wanda, again in 1963 with Mary, and again in 1971 with Mary. Magical. It was worth the attempts. Midge, lift the wine. Let us toast . . . it is coming to a close, and we made it . . . by hook or by crook.